# THE ASIAN CRISIS TURNS GLOBAL

**Manuel F. Montes**
**Vladimir V. Popov**



ISEAS
INSTITUTE OF SOUTHEAST ASIAN STUDIES

Published by
Institute of Southeast Asian Studies
30 Heng Mui Keng Terrace
Pasir Panjang
Singapore 119614

*Internet e-mail*: publish@iseas.edu.sg
*World Wide Web*: http://www.iseas.edu.sg/pub.html


First reprint 1999



**Cataloguing in Publication Data**

Montes, Manuel F.
The Asian crisis turns global / by Manuel F. Montes and Vladimir V. Popov.
(ISEAS current economic affairs series, 0218-2114)
1. Financial crises—Asia.
2. Financial crises—Russia (Federation)
3. Asia—Economic conditions.
4. Capital market.
5. International economic relations.
V. Popov, Vladimir, 1954-
VI. Title.
VIII. Series.
HG5770.5 A3M77 1999 sls99-9079

ISBN 981-230-050-3
ISSN 0218-2114

Typeset by Superskill Graphics Pte Ltd
Printed in Singapore by Seng Lee Press Pte Ltd

# THE ASIAN CRISIS TURNS GLOBAL

The **Institute of Southeast Asian Studies (ISEAS)** was established as an autonomous organization in 1968. It is a regional research centre for scholars and other specialists concerned with modern Southeast Asia, particularly the many-faceted problems of stability and security, economic development, and political and social change.

The Institute's research programmes are the Regional Economic Studies (RES, including ASEAN and APEC), Regional Strategic and Political Studies (RSPS), Regional Social and Cultural Studies (RSCS), and the ASEAN Transitional Economies Programme (ATEP).

The Institute is governed by a twenty-two-member Board of Trustees comprising nominees from the Singapore Government, the National University of Singapore, the various Chambers of Commerce, and professional and civic organizations. A ten-man Executive Committee oversees day-to-day operations; it is chaired by the Director, the Institute's chief academic and administrative officer.

# Contents

# List of Tables

# List of Figures

# 1
# INTRODUCTION

On 17 August 1998, the Asian currency crisis, which started in mid-1997, metastasized into a global financial crisis with the devaluation of the rouble and a declaration of a Russian government default on its internal debt. Of the succession of national currency crises that began with the devaluation of the Thai baht on 2 July 1997, Russia's crisis may yet prove to be the most far reaching in economic, political, and international terms.

The direct impact of the Russian economic crisis itself was a significant seizing up of international finance to emerging economies. In the month after the crisis, interest rate premia on emerging economy bonds shot up to unprecedented levels of 10 to 15 percentage points. As private finance dried up for developing countries, net capital funds gushed out of emerging economies into safe haven industrial economy financial markets. Brazil experienced a loss in reserves of $28 billion after the Russian crisis. On 13 November 1998, Brazil accepted a $42 billion dollar programme as a way to stave off a currency devaluation. This programme failed on 13 January 1999 when Brazil devalued its currency, the *real*. Overvalued exchange rates, soaring fiscal deficits, and surging capital outflows were shared features of the Russian and Brazilian crises.

While the Russian crisis of August 1998 was perhaps the most spectacular example, there have actually been currency crises in other transition economies. The Russian crisis was preceded by currency crises in Bulgaria and Romania in 1996, in Ukraine and Belarus in 1997–98 and followed by a still unfolding currency crisis in Kyrgyzstan in November 1998.

One common feature among the list of countries that have fallen victim to the crisis is that these countries have been the "darlings of international finance". Before the financial crisis of 1997, international investors had poured money into the stock markets in the affected East Asian economies, Latin America, Russia and Eastern Europe and bought the limited supply of domestic bonds available. Investor interest encouraged a flurry of new bond and equity flotations, both domestically and in foreign markets, and the start-up of new financial ventures in these countries.

The East Asian economies (most particularly Indonesia, Thailand, Malaysia, Singapore, and Korea) have been touted as having staged the East Asian "miracle" (World Bank 1993) of development based on high domestic savings and successful export strategies. Beginning in the mid-1980s, these East Asian economies carried out successive programmes to liberalize their trade regimes (Montes 1997). In 1988 or so, the same countries carried out accelerated efforts to liberalize their domestic financial systems and in the 1990s to liberalize rules on external investments. When the crisis began in 1997, these countries had for the most part achieved capital account convertibility.

The transition economies in Eastern Europe and the new states from the former Soviet Union (FSU) also generated immense investor interest. In this case, however, in terms of quantity, private sector investment has been more modest. The inflow of foreign direct investment (FDI) in 1989–96 to Russia amounted to some $5 billion. This is equivalent to only about 1 per cent of its annual GDP, as compared to 30 per cent of GDP in Hungary and China, and 5–15 per cent in Albania, Azerbaijan, Czech Republic, Estonia, Hungary, Kazakhstan, Latvia and Turkmenistan during the same period (EBRD 1997, p.12; World Bank 1996, p.64). Only in Bulgaria, Czech Republic and Slovakia, Hungary, Turkmenistan and Vietnam did the short-term debt to GDP ratio exceed 7 per cent in 1996.

Nevertheless, despite the modest absolute dimensions of capital inflows into transition economies, the impact of these inflows on many of them was quite dramatic. A few years earlier, before the transition started, the then communist countries were completely closed to international investment into domestic securities (attracting foreign capital only in the form of bank or government credits). In Russia, for instance, the stock market, fuelled by the inflows of foreign capital, grew in the year 1997 alone by three (!) times in dollar terms and became the best performing emerging market for that year. Similarly, the Russian government attracted significant external private credit, issuing foreign exchange denominated Eurobonds and rouble denominated short-term securities (a third of which was purchased by foreign investors); these resources were financing over half of the total government budget deficit before the crisis.

Even though the European transition economies had just emerged from central planning, institutional weaknesses in domestic financial markets did not seem to unduly restrict private interest, as has also been the case for other emerging economies. The capital inflows these countries elicited were based on international perceptions that they were liberalizing their trade rapidly and achieving significant progress in eliminating their foreign investment restrictions.

This crisis has chosen to afflict the very countries that have depended most heavily on the international economy for their economic growth and in the case of the East Asian economies had been seen to have achieved some success in integrating their economies with international markets. This suggests the decisive influence of the international dimension in the currency crises which are the main burden of this book.

One might say that these crises could be the first wave of such crises the world will see in the future. Were these crises only the result of financial contagion spreading in the global economy? Could these series of crises be attributed to domestic causes? If these causes were purely domestic, does the coincidence of crises justify the view that the causes of the crises in East Asia and in Russia and other transition economies are similar in nature? We argue that neither of the above explanations is true and in fact embrace a third explanation: currency crises in transition economies resulted mostly from domestic policy mistakes, but of a different nature than those in Southeast Asia.

We believe that currency crises in post-communist countries may be best explained by "first generation" currency crisis models, i.e., by straightforward macroeconomic mismanagement — overvaluation of the exchange rates before the crises. In Russia, the crisis was aggravated by the decision to default on the short-term, and later long-term, debt, which was by no means necessary, i.e., the Russian debt crisis was artificially manufactured by the government. On the contrary, in East Asia currencies were not overvalued, macroeconomic policy was generally prudent and economic fundamentals were sound. The collapse of these currencies became the side effect of the private sector debt crisis, as the culmination of the private over-extension of credit by banks and companies financed by foreign borrowing.

Our analysis leads us to conclude that the currency crises in transition economies were in a sense less complicated than those in Southeast Asian countries and that there is much more to be learned by transition economies from Southeast Asian experience than the other way around. Or, to put it differently, all lessons from the recent global experience with the currency crises seem to be relevant for the transition economies, whereas for Asian countries their own experience with currency crises seems to be more challenging in policy and theoretical terms than the experience of other countries.

Risking oversimplification, we may state that transition economies only repeated the most obvious macroeconomic management mistakes that were made more than once by other countries before and thus tell us the story that is only too familiar — the appreciation of the real exchange rate resulting from the combination of the nominal exchange rate peg and the ongoing inflation; the deterioration of the current account and the outflow of capital in the anticipation of the devaluation; the depletion of the foreign exchange reserves and the subsequent currency collapse. The Asian story is more complex and, as explained later, caught many economists by surprise. Exchange rates were not egregiously overvalued; there were prudent government macroeconomic policies with limited budget deficits and no significant government debt, and yet a full fledged currency crisis occurred rooted in a private sector debt crisis after a period of unsustainable credit expansion.

The lessons to be learned from the currency crises in transition economies are about the consistency of macroeconomic policy goals and the efficiency of different macroeconomic stabilization programmes. Perhaps, the most important lesson is that the exchange rate (which is said to be the single most important price in an open market economy) is far too important for use solely for fighting inflation (which is exactly what was tried by some post-communist countries).

The recent experience of East Asian countries highlights the possibility of widespread failures on the part of the private sector to properly assess risk and undertake the appropriate level of lending and borrowing. It suggests an unavoidable role for appropriate government regulations which set not only the rules of the game, but also strongly encourage prudent behaviour. The East Asian lesson seems to be that the process of carrying the "twin liberalizations" (that of capital account and that of domestic financial system) is fraught with enormous risk, if carried out haphazardly and simultaneously.

We set for ourselves as a first objective of accurate characterizing of these crises to the extent possible. *It is important to diagnose the reasons for the disease before prescribing the medicine* — to correctly identify domestic causes and to distinguish these from external causes. In the concluding chapter of this book, we set out the lessons for domestic policy that these cases have suggested and a set of suggestions for reforming international capital markets.

# 2
# CURRENCY CRISES
# Theories and Typologies

Currency crises are as old as currencies themselves. Currency crises occurred even when central banks did not yet exist and banknotes issued by the commercial banks were the major means of exchange. A currency is thrown into a crisis when it is subjected to a drastic drop in value (relative to other assets) as a result of sudden loss of confidence from its holders. In a world where access to alternative monies exists,[1] abrupt currency devaluations and the rapid depletion of reserves are the surest manifestations of a currency crisis.

Why do currency crises occur? It is useful to distinguish between currency crises or foreign exchange crises *per se* and the more complicated cases of debt and credit (banking) crises. The latter two types — credit and debt crises — can themselves provoke a currency crisis but the original cause would be different.

## Collapse of an Unsustainable Currency Peg

The first type of crisis — a foreign exchange (currency) crisis — can occur even without international capital flows, creditors, lenders and banks. The only necessary precondition for the currency collapse (an abrupt change in the exchange rate) is a peg of the exchange rate by the central bank or attempts to maintain the flexible rate (dirty float) at an unsustainable level. If a country's policies — monetary, fiscal, or trade — are too different from those of its neighbours or key trading partners, the demand for and the supply of foreign exchange move grossly out-of-line with equilibrium at the targeted rate. Downward or upward pressure on the currency emerges, and this subsequently leads to a devaluation/revaluation of the exchange rate. An external debt crisis, although not a necessary precondition of such currency collapses, often accompanies such crises since much of the funding used to maintain the unsustainable exchange rate had often been obtained from foreign parties.

In the case of a downward pressure on the currency, the ability of the central bank to defend it is limited by the level of foreign exchange reserves. Maintaining international reserves is not costless for developing countries. These resources, which have to be invested in foreign currencies, would normally earn higher returns in the domestic market and could be used to fund domestic investment. This is why reserves are usually limited to at most several months of import payments and several days of capital outflows.

In the case of upward pressure on the currency, the central bank can defend the level of the exchange rate by building up foreign exchange reserves. This ability is constrained by the inevitable inflationary consequences of a swelling money supply, as a result of foreign exchange purchases by the monetary authorities to prevent the exchange rate from appreciating. An alternative policy, sterilization, can be costly and self-defeating. Sterilization consists of reversing the monetary infusions occasioned by the foreign exchange purchases through the sale of domestic bonds at generous interest rates. Sterilization policies impose additional fiscal deficits[2] and often lead to higher interest rates (and to even more upward pressure on the currency by provoking new capital inflows).

Once a drastic devaluation or revaluation occurs, shifts in

relative prices and terms of trade may provoke a supply side recession. It also inflicts large capital gains/losses in assets and liabilities denominated in foreign currency. These devaluations/revaluations have also caused disruptions in the repayment of credits (debt and banking crises).

The degree of the unsustainability of the currency peg depends on the extent to which monetary, fiscal, or trade deficits are cumulatively "inconsistent" with the exchange rate. In these so-called "first generation" models, currency attacks are justified by chronic flow deficits. In Krugman's (1979) model, speculators, observing the pattern of falling international reserves, "short" the currency by borrowing in the domestic currency and immediately converting the proceeds into foreign currencies. By taking these asset positions, speculators draw upon ("attack") a finite level of international reserves. They promise to sell the domestic currency in the near future when its value relative to foreign currencies has fallen, deriving their profits from the cheaper price of the domestic currency.

Speculators profit from the eventual currency devaluation when the reserves run out, an eventuality precipitated by the "shorting" operation itself. The origin of the crisis is therefore "a fundamental inconsistency between domestic policies — typically the persistence of money-financed budget deficits — and the attempt to maintain a fixed exchange rate" (Krugman 1979).

The standard flow deficit mechanism as first enunciated in the Polak (1957) model (which subsequently served as the basis for International Monetary Fund adjustment programmes) was that public sector deficits lay behind unsustainable current account deficits. Because of the state's weak fiscal performance and its unmatched influence over monetary policy, the financing of these domestic deficits also had a large reliance on liquidity creation. The solution to such a crisis is to drastically reduce the fiscal deficit and tighten monetary liquidity.

A key argument developed in this paper is that the Russian crisis of August 1998 precisely follows the pattern of a first generation crisis, a straightforward "plain vanilla" currency crisis caused by the overvaluation of the national currency. Since the introduction of a crawling peg system for the rouble in mid-1995, the exchange rate has been overvalued, inducing, first, an export growth slowdown followed by export growth stagnation, while imports continued to rise. As a result, even though Russia is an important international supplier of a diverse set of international commodities, the current account surplus has shrunk and turned negative in the first half of 1998, at which time capital outflow accelerated in the face of a possible devaluation.

These balance of payments trends steadily depleted Russia's foreign exchange reserves, which have never been large ($15 billion in the beginning of 1998 or about two months of imports). At the end of July 1998, Russia received the first tranche of $4 billion under the emergency credits from the International Monetary Fund (IMF). These new resources were exhausted in about three weeks as the capital flight continued and the rouble devaluation followed on 17 August. We shall explain subsequently how clumsy government policies with regard to Russian debt obligations needlessly aggravated the crisis and have complicated the prospects for economic recovery.

### External Debt Crises — Government and Private

A second type of the currency crisis is the one that is brought about by a debt crisis with foreign creditors. Because most credit relationships are presumed to be ongoing relationships, such crises reflect an unexpected breakdown in the credit relationship, such as a sudden loss of confidence on the part of lenders on the borrower's ability to pay or an unwillingness on the part of borrowers to service current obligations. We can make a distinction between two kinds of debt-provoked currency crises on the basis of the dominant borrowing party: (a) a government debt crisis if the breakdown is over government external debt and (b) a private debt crisis if the breakdown is over private external debt.

A perceived unwillingness or inability of a government to honour its external debt obligations occasions a government debt crisis. If the debts are denominated in foreign currency, like Mexican *Tesobonos* in 1994, the connection is obvious: the outflow of capital in the expectation of the default and/or devaluation leads to reserve depletion and triggers a devaluation. If the obligations are denominated in domestic currency, investors, afraid of the inflationary financing of the public deficits (leading to inflation and devaluation), switch to foreign exchange. The Mexican peso in 1994 and many Latin American currencies in the early 1980s were undermined by exactly this kind of mechanism. The outflow of capital caused by the mistrust in the ability of the government to pay back their debts brought down even those currencies in Latin America that were strong and not overvalued.

Currencies can be attacked on the basis of the pattern of accumulating government debt or on the expectation that government debt will balloon in the future when political pressures make it impossible to continue to balance the budget especially when unemployment in high. "Second-generation" models[3] justify a currency attack not from fundamental weaknesses, but from predictions that government policy must become more expansionary in the future in order to satisfy political demands for lower unemployment and faster growth.

These models are interesting because they identify multiple

equilibria and the possibility that economies can be pushed into a disastrous equilibria because of changes in policy and/or market sentiment (Montes 1998*a*). Second-generation models also provide an analytical description of self-fulfilling behaviour on the part of market participants that could be quite out of line with observed fundamentals. These models had to be invented in response to the 1992 crisis of the European Exchange Rate Mechanism (ERM) which erupted in a situation of strong fundamentals but still succeeded in forcing the UK and Italy out of the exchange rate arrangement.

Krugman (1997) argues that currency crises caused by mounting accumulation of debt are covered by "so called second generation models". These models assume that the governments weigh the costs and benefits of abandoning the peg: once investors realize that the advantages of the depreciation of the debt denominated in domestic currency are greater than the disadvantages associated with devaluation, they attack the currency and the crisis breaks out.

A private-debt-induced currency crisis originates from a perceived inability or unwillingness of the domestic private sector to service its external debt obligations. This is the type of the currency crisis that erupted, with such unexpected virulence, in 1997 in many Southeast Asian economies. The best example among the Asian countries is the Indonesian case. Before the Asian economic crisis, 50 per cent of the total Indonesian external debt was private and 79 per cent of the private external debt had been borrowed directly by Indonesian corporations[4] instead of through the domestic banking system. Even if Indonesia escaped a domestic banking crisis (which it did not), it certainly would have had a private external debt crisis.

The Asian currency crises share many of the features of a

generalized run on domestic currency assets based on imperfect information about weaknesses in the domestic financial systems of the afflicted economies (Montes 1998*a*, p.52). A key role of the financial sector is to undertake maturity and currency transformation. However, if there were a panic of withdrawals, there would not be enough resources to satisfy all the demands. This fact, along with the limited level of international reserves being held by public authorities, provided the certainty that in such a situation there would not be sufficient funds to cover short-term obligations. The features of a bank run, modelled in equilibrium terms by Diamond and Dybvig (1983), would thus apply.[5]

Krugman (1998) describes the currency crises in Asia as "only part of a broader financial crisis, which had very little to do with currencies or even monetary issues per se. Nor did the crisis have much to do with the traditional fiscal issues" but rather was related to issues "normally neglected in the currency crisis analysis: the role of financial intermediaries (and the moral hazard associated with such intermediaries when they are poorly regulated), and the prices of real assets such as capital and land". The Asian story, he continues, is not a problem brought about by fiscal deficits, as in "first generation models", nor is one brought on by macroeconomic temptation, as in "second generation models". The Asian crises derived from sudden losses of confidence in the overvalued assets of the financial system and saw the subsequent collapses of asset values in general, with the currency crises more of a symptom than a cause of this underlying real malady.

## Domestic Credit Originated Currency Crises

The third general origin of a currency crisis, which we might call a "domestic credit-induced" crisis, is closely related to a private external debt crisis. We suggest it as a separate type to underline the interaction, drawn from lessons from the Asian economic crisis, within the "twin liberalizations" (Kaminsky and Reinhart 1996): liberalizing the domestic financial system and liberalizing external financial flows. The origin for this type is a systemic crisis in the domestic banking system; unlike the immediately previous type the origin is purely domestic and it does not originate with a breakdown of the credit relationship between the domestic private borrowers and international lenders. Such a crisis sparks an attempted flight from domestic financial assets, due to the perceptions of weaknesses in the domestic banking system (Montes 1998*b*) and the unwillingness of domestic investors to keep their savings in the domestic financial system.

If external financial flows are liberalized, financial assets will flow out the country in response to such a domestic credit crisis, provoking a currency crisis; if they are not, a systemic credit crisis in the domestic banking does not have to lead to a currency crisis.

In East Asia, China provides the best example of an economy where there did exist a significantly weakened domestic financial system; estimates of as high as 40 to 50 per cent of banking assets being non-performing were being reported even before the Asian crisis ignited. However, through the period of the crisis, China's international reserves remained stable and the Chinese renminbi had not succumbed — as of January 1999 — to pressures to follow the devaluation of the currencies in the region because China had not yet liberalized its capital account (i.e., cross-border transactions in financial investments).

Nevertheless, there are indications of significant capital flight from China, even though both its nature and magnitude — in the context of China's substantial international reserves — does not yet seem be hazardous. It appears that the repatriation of foreign exchange earnings back to China has unmistakably fallen during the global financial crisis. The evidence is indirect: despite a monthly trade surplus of nearly $4 billion and the inflow of foreign investment of over $3 billion (*Financial Post*, 29 September 1998) foreign exchange reserves have not increased at all. This indicates that "capital flight" in the form of a reduction of repatriated earnings accelerated in 1998 and reached $60 billion in the previous twelve-month period. If China did not have capital controls, such a pattern could have easily included the depletion of its foreign exchange reserves.

## Interaction between Types of Currency Crises

The suggested classification is of course a rough scheme, since every particular currency crisis is caused by a variety of factors and usually combines the features of all three types of mechanisms. Sachs, Tornell and Velasco (1996) examine the predictive power of three indicators. The first is real currency appreciation which is an indicator of the overvaluation of the exchange rate in our terminology. The second is the ratio of M2 to foreign exchange reserves, which can be interpreted as a measure of the indebtedness of the public sector. The third is the strength of recent lending booms, which for the most part indicates the indebtedness of the private sector. They find that out of twenty examined emerging market economies those that were particularly hard hit by the 1994–95 crisis (Mexico, Argentina, Brazil) displayed in the preceding period not only rather low reserve ratios, but experienced strong real appreciation of currencies and lending booms. Similarly, the rapid growth in the ratio of bank credit to GDP preceded earlier financial troubles in Argentina (1981), Chile (1981–82), Colombia (1982–83), Uruguay (1982), Norway (1987), Finland (1991–92), Japan (1992–93) and Sweden (1991).

Because of economic structures and patterns in the reform process, there is a rich set of interactions between the different origins of currency crises we have presented.

One important interaction is that in which the private sector debt originated currency crisis intersects with the domestic credit-induced crisis. The interaction here is between the domestic financial system (which in the case of the emerging economies is dominated by banks augmented by small equity and bond markets) and the international financial system.

This interaction has been heightened precisely by the "twin liberalizations" and it is important in understanding the Asian economic crises. Before these crises, Kaminsky and Reinhart (1996) examined 71 balance-of-payments crises and 25 banking crises during the period 1970–95. While there were only 3 banking crises associated with the 25 balance-of-payments crises during 1970–79, 22 banking crises coincided with 46 payments crises over 1980–95. In their view, financial liberalization (which occurred mostly after 1980) appears to play a significant role in explaining the probability of a banking crisis preceded by a private lending boom. In turn, a banking crisis helps to predict a currency crisis.

The domestic credit lending boom in the two previous crises — in the Southern Cone economies of Latin America (Chile, Argentina, and Uruguay) of 1981–82 and in the Scandinavian economies (Norway, Sweden, and Finland) in 1987–92 — as was the case in the Southeast Asian economies had been fed by the inflow of foreign funds.

This interaction between the domestic banking system and international finance brings up the role of national governments in supervising their domestic banking systems. What is involved here is that national authorities have an abiding interest in maintaining the viability of their domestic banking system. Because of this abiding interest, national governments can be seen by markets to be obligated to guarantee the liabilities of their domestic banks, whether or not there is an explicit promise to do so.

National governments are therefore subject to potentially large contingent liabilities should drastic changes in the macroeconomic situation endanger the soundness of their domestic banking system, even when all the parties involved are private. National authorities in the East Asian economies (especially Thailand, Indonesia, and Korea) and in Russia have had to wrestle with the soaring of these claims on government resources to help to prevent a meltdown of the domestic banking system after the crisis began.

Under the so-called "Lawson doctrine", named after the UK Chancellor of the Exchequer Nigel Lawson in the Thatcher government who proclaimed it in September 1988, the government need to care only about "its own fundamentals", i.e., about its own indebtedness and about public sector budget deficits. If current account deficits and the accumulation of external debts result purely from the activities of the private sector, which was the case in the UK before its 1989 crisis and in Thailand before its 1997 crisis, it should be of no concern to the government.

The implicit assumption in the doctrine is that market pressures will force private actors to become eventually more prudent in their credit activities. For example, when a country's short-term external borrowing has increased beyond the level of its international reserves, the cost at which it borrows should increase because of the higher risk of default. This assumption, that the costs of risky lending will be internalized by the private sector, has proven to be wrong in the period before the Asian crisis. The premium on lending to Thailand and other East Asian economies continued to decline and credit ratings continued to improve up to day of the eruption of the crisis.

The East Asian crises were neither purely foreign exchange

(balance of payments) crises, nor government debt crises (which induced currency crises). With certain qualifications, these economies had strong fundamentals: high saving ratios, strong growth, undervalued rather than overvalued currencies, low inflation, government budget surpluses and low government debt. It was exactly the excessive borrowing of the private sector abroad (banks in Thailand, industrial companies in Indonesia, chaebols in Korea) that caused the mistrust of investors and resulted in the outflow of capital and the currency crises.

A further important interaction is that between pegged exchange rates and private external borrowing and this interaction also involves the role of the national government. When Thailand devalued the baht in July 1997 its international reserves had shrunk to about $1.4 billion from a previously reported level of $31 billion. In the year before the crisis, Thailand's current account deficit was 8.1 per cent of its GDP.[6] One might diagnose Thailand's currency crisis as simply the result of an unsustainable peg, a first generation crisis just as we have suggested is the case for the Russian crisis.

Even though the Thai baht had indeed appreciated before the crisis, these had been quite modest when measured using conventional indices.[7] Such a modest appreciation cannot explain the depth of the Thai crisis. We shall argue that overvaluation of the currency was not an important origin in discussing the East Asian cases, though it was very important in the case of transition economies, and especially in the Russian case.

However, the strong currency pegs in the East Asian economies sent a signal to international lenders that their loans to these economies were not subject to the risk of the devaluation of the currency. This played a key role in both weakening the domestic financial system and abetting the rapid buildup of private external debt — setting the stage for two of the kinds of currency crises we have presented.

If financial markets are working as idealized and given (a) that inflation rates in the Southeast Asian countries have been low (Montes 1998*a*), (b) that government deficits were not only low they were declining (Montes 1998*a*) and (c) that sovereign premia were declining right up to day the crisis began, the strict currency pegs should have led to a convergence of domestic with international interest rates (a reduction in interest differentials). However, interest differentials, instead of declining, remained significant. The interest differentials provided the strong pull factor for private borrowing from abroad. Reisen (1998) suggests that reasons behind the unyielding differentials had already been detected in connection with the Southern Cone banking crises of the 1980s. The main culprits were identified to be domestic market imperfections and oligopolistic structures. For example, large domestic conglomerates (*grupos economicos* in Chile and *conglomerasi* in Indonesia) have favoured access to lower interest rate loans from abroad while other domestic enterprises have to be rationed through high interest domestic loans. The impact of the maintained interest differential is soaring external private debt cum domestic lending boom.

# 3
# EXCHANGE RATES IN DEVELOPING AND TRANSITION ECONOMIES

In the theoretical literature, there are well-articulated views that suggest that, in contrast to mature industrial market economies, developing countries and transition economies may experience prolonged periods of real exchange rate appreciation. In practice, a tendency towards real exchange rate appreciation would be a cause of concern in a developing economy seeking to strengthen the competitiveness of its exports in overseas markets and for a transition economy striving to protect its domestic industries from competition from imported products. The real appreciation of the currency may also lead to a balance-of-payments crisis.

## Tendencies towards Currency Appreciation in Emerging Economies

For developing countries, the Balassa-Samuelson effect is one suggested explanation for a long term tendency of real appreciation of national currencies. If productivity grows faster in the traded than in non-traded goods sector,[8] and if wage rates are equalized across sectors with the result that real wage increases lag behind productivity growth, then the real exchange rate can appreciate without undermining business profits. How the Asian export-oriented economies have dealt with this theoretical tendency and responded to the real world challenges of obtaining market shares in overseas markets is an important part of the story behind the exchange and monetary policies that had been in place before the Asian crisis.

For transition economies, however, an explanation that relies on lagging productivity growth in the non-tradeable sector is hardly feasible. The non-traded goods sector (services) was unquestionably underdeveloped before transition and thus became the fastest growing sector after transition.[9] At the start of the transition, the non-trade sectors showed stronger productivity gains than the traded goods sector.

Given that the transition process is supposed to be a finite (though perhaps a drawn-out) process, real exchange appreciation after the initial fixing of the nominal rate against international currencies might simply be a case of temporary maladjustment as has been the case when non-transition economies have loosened their pegs until more normal volumes of market transactions allow a more sustainable exchange rate based on the economy's overall competitiveness. For the transition economies, Halpern and Wyplosz (1997), however, explain the appreciation of real exchange rate not only by traditional initial overshooting (undervaluation of national currencies when establishing convertibility), but also by the nature of the transformation process itself.

Grafe and Wyplosz (1997) suggest an alternative to the Balassa-Samuelson effect, based on model in which the real exchange rates alters the distribution of revenues between labor and firms. Real appreciation sets in as the need for capital accumulation financed by savings declines. This model may capture an important stylized fact about transition — the decline in the ratio of investment to GDP, which was abnormally high in the centrally planned economies due to the need to compensate for low capital productivity (Shmelev and Popov 1989). In virtually all transition economies investment/GDP ratios initially fell, and even after recovery have not reached the levels that existed before reforms (Popov 1998*a*). However, in most transition economies the decline in investment/GDP ratios has already come to an end so that the impact of this factor on real exchange rate trends cannot be expected to last.

Halpern and Wyplosz (1997), nevertheless, argue that real appreciation in transition economies will continue until the transition is over (which may according to them be "decades away"). They conclude that any attempts to resist real appreciation are not only hopeless, but can lead to potentially speculative capital inflows. Capital inflows, if not sterilized, lead to faster money growth and eventually inflation. If capital inflows are sterilized, there can be a buildup of reserves fueling further inflows in an unending spiral. Even more destabilizing, from their vantage point, would be a policy of nominal depreciation, for example, based on the purchasing power parity (PPP) rule, which leads to a dangerous cycle of inflation and depreciation.

## East Asian versus the Transition Economy Stance on Exchange Rate Management

It is worth noting that the exchange rate stances before the crisis of the East Asian countries were decisively directed at resisting real appreciation in order to defend their export competitiveness. For the countries that elicited the most ferocious interest from foreign investors, such as Thailand, Malaysia and Indonesia, the effort could best be described as trying to avoid steep real exchange rate appreciations. Montes (1998*a*, pp.20–21) describes the Thai dilemma thus:

> In regard to macroeconomic management, between 1990 and 1995, one might almost describe the Thai public authorities effort as one of a gallant rearguard action in the face of enormous offers of portfolio financing seeking to participate in Thailand's development prospects. One

> might have thought that with such a volume of inflow, the real exchange rate would have appreciated significantly, further weakening the export sector. Thailand has managed to maintain a baht real exchange rate remarkably close to its 1990 level (Bond 1997 p.8). Thai inflation rates have also been low during the period. While central bank operations everywhere can only be observed indirectly, this achievement entailed enormous leaning against wind. First, as already shown above, the public sector generated surpluses to offset the demand effects of the capital inflow. Second, there would have been substantial sterilization operations at significant costs in terms of quasi-public deficits. Thailand engaged in periodic and significant sterilization operations in defense of its real exchange rate, that is, against its appreciation. Suggestions that the baht should have been depreciated earlier would have required accepting higher public deficits from an even greater measure of sterilization.

We shall explain in detail later how such policies exacerbated the unstable growth path the capital inflow episode had induced.

The view that the real exchange rate in transition economies is doomed to appreciate is a good starting point for the discussion of the currency crises in the region. True, one of the basic stylized facts about exchange rates in transition economies is the substantial appreciation of the real exchange rate after deregulation of prices and introduction of the convertibility. Of major East European (EE) and FSU economies, only in Slovenia was the real exchange relatively stable, whereas in all the other countries there was a more or less prolonged (several years) period of real appreciation of national currencies.

However, in most countries real appreciation had slowed down by the mid-1990s and in some it stopped completely. Moreover, in 1996–98 five post-communist countries with previously rapidly appreciating real exchange rates (Bulgaria, Romania, Belarus, Russia and Ukraine — in chronological order) have witnessed the collapse of their currencies (Figure 3.1). In all five countries the brisk devaluation of the currencies was no less significant than those in Asia in 1997–98 (with the exception of Indonesia, where the rupiah at one point lost 80 per cent of its value) and no less significant than in Mexico in 1994–95. In fact, in Bulgaria and Russia, where currencies depreciated by nearly two-thirds, the size of the depreciations was quite significant, and in Belarus — even more significant than in Indonesia. (See Figures 3.1 and 3.2.)

Why have these currency crises occurred? Had the real appreciation of currencies before the crisis in these countries gone too far? We argue that the answer to the above question is positive and that the over-appreciation of exchange rates should be held responsible for the crises in the transition economies.

First of all, none of the economic crises in the transition economies can be traced to external debt distress whether government or private. Using conventional measures of country indebtedness to compare the situation *vis-à-vis* Latin American countries, post-communist governments were not considerably indebted. Using the same benchmarks and comparing these with Southeast Asian countries, companies and banks in former centrally planned economies (CPE) did not manage to accumulate sizeable debts.

Most communist governments were quite prudent in accumulating external debts. Moreover, most of the former Communist countries began their transition without any accumulated debt. Except for Russia which had assumed all the debts of the Soviet Union, the newly created FSU states started their existence with no indebtedness at all, while for Poland and several other East European countries

FIGURE 3.1

**Exchange Rates in Transition Economies (National currencies per $1, January 1997=100%)**

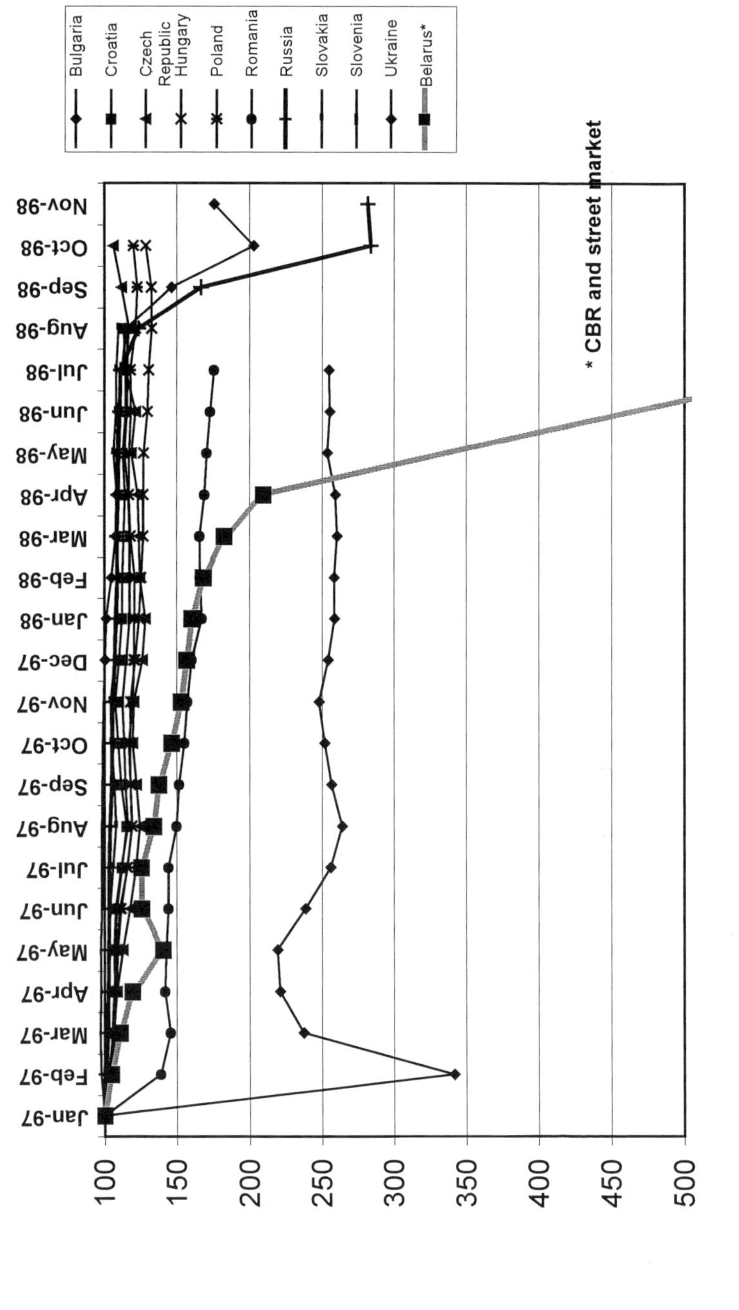

FIGURE 3.2

**Exchange Rates in Southeast Asia (National currencies per $1, Jan. 1997=100%) and in Mexico (Jan. 1994=100%)**

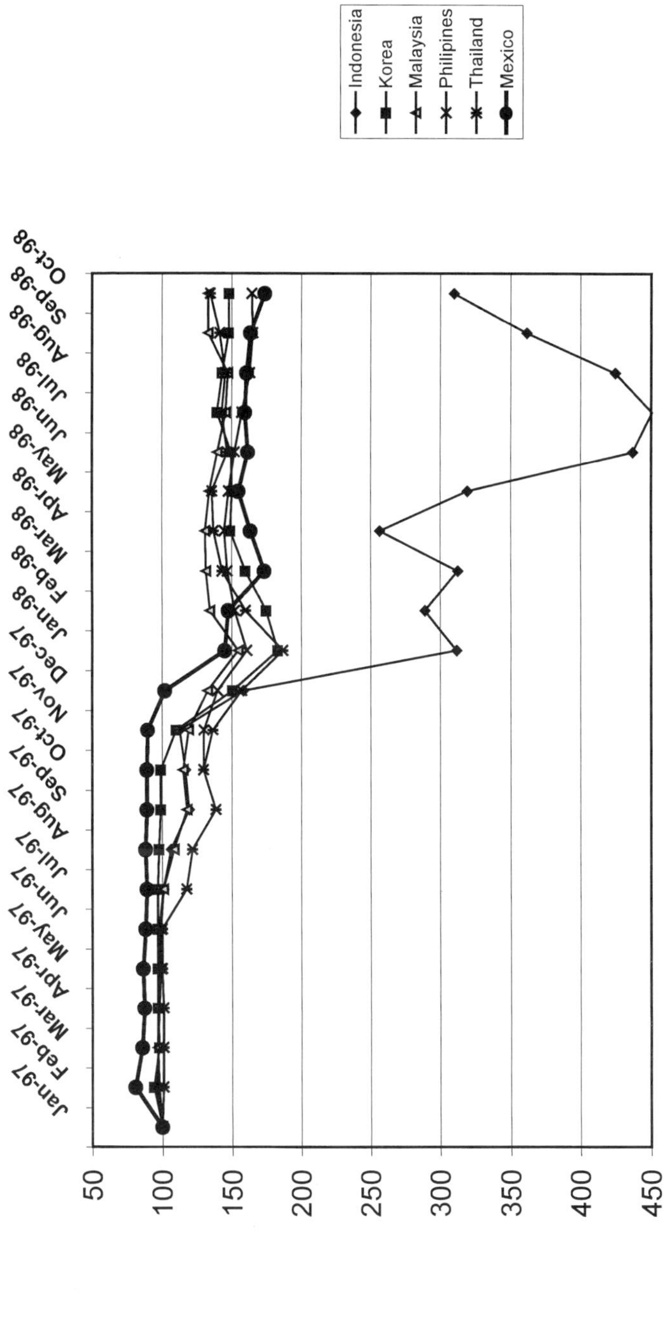


SOURCE: International financial statistics and Central Bank of Russia

external debts were restructured and partly written off.[10] On the other hand, companies and banks in transition economies (which under CPE had not been allowed to borrow abroad) did not have much of a credit history and had just been starting to accumulate foreign debts when the Asian crisis broke out in July 1997.

As Table 3.1 suggests, only in four transition economies (Bulgaria, Hungary, Mongolia and Vietnam) did the foreign debt-to-GDP ratios exceed 60 per cent. Even in these economies, however, debt service payments were quite low (because of debt restructuring), so that in no transition economy did debt service payments exceed 20 per cent of the export of goods and services in 1996 (except for Bulgaria which was 20.5 per cent). By way of comparison, debt service payments amounted to 30–40 per cent of export revenues for major Latin American countries, and to 20–30 per cent for the largest Asian developing economies. Short-term debt in transition states was relatively low as compared to total foreign debt, whereas foreign exchange reserves in most cases substantially exceeded the outstanding short-term indebtedness (Table 3.1).

In three of the seven post-communist countries that experienced the currency crises (Belarus, Bulgaria and Russia) international reserves were barely enough to cover the short-term debt, which obviously created an additional crisis potential. However, in Romania and Ukraine, Georgia and Kyrgyztan, all debt indicators were at safe levels, so their crises appear by and large as purely exchange rate crises. We contend that in Belarus, Bulgaria, and especially in Russia, the exchange rate overvaluation was most likely the major reason for the crisis as well.

The undervaluation of domestic currency, as conventionally reflected in low ratios of the nominal exchange rate to its purchasing power parity is an often-seen feature for most developing and transition countries. These countries normally need to earn a trade surplus to finance debt service payments and capital flight.[11] Unlike in mature market economies, in most poorer countries the exchange rates of national currencies is low as compared to PPP (Table 3.2). For resource-rich countries, however, there is a danger of the "Dutch disease," which arises because resource exports are so profitable that it allows a developing country to earn a trade surplus even under an overpriced (overvalued) exchange rate. Thus, Middle East countries (mostly oil exporters) are the only major group of states in the developing world with the exchange rate close to PPP (Table 3.2).

On the other hand, many other developing countries (including those rich in resources) pursue a conscious policy of undervalued exchange rates as part of their general export orientation strategy. By creating a downward pressure on their currencies through the building up foreign exchange reserves, they are able to limit consumption and imports and to stimulate exports, investment, and growth.

The strategy of maintaining an undervalued exchange rate[12] had been successfully deployed by Japan, Korea, Taiwan and Singapore in their development process, when these countries were still poor and were catching up with high income states. This is currently the strategy of many new emerging market economies, especially that of China, which continues to keep the exchange rate at an extremely low level (five times lower than PPP rate) by accumulating foreign exchange reserves at a record pace. It is by no means an accident that all very fast growing economies are also famous for high and rapidly growing international reserves: China (including Hong Kong), Taiwan, Singapore, Malaysia, Thailand, account for a good 20 per cent of total world reserves. The reserves-to-GDP ratio for these countries is normally above 20 per cent, compared to only 8 per cent for the world as a whole (World Bank 1997).

There is an obvious link between the undervaluation of

TABLE 3.1
**External Indebtedness and Reserves in Selected Transition Economies, Asian and Latin American Countries, 1996**
(In percentages)

| *Country* | *Debt/ GDP* | *Debt service payments / Export of goods and services* | *Short term debt / Total debt* | *Reserves / GDP* | *Reserves / Short term debt* |
|---|---|---|---|---|---|
| | | **Transition economies** | | | |
| **Albania** | 32 | 3.5 | 7 | 12.5 | 536 |
| **Armenia** | 27 | 10.7 | 0.3 | 11.6 | 14265 |
| **Azerbaijan** | 10 | 1.3 | 3.6 | 5.8 | 1606 |
| **Belarus** | 21 | 2 | 9.5 | 2.4 | 122 |
| **Bosnia and Herzegovina** | 53 | – | – | – | – |
| **Bulgaria** | 89 | 20.5 | 9.2 | 9 | 111 |
| **China** | 17 | 8.7 | 19.7 | 13.7 | 409 |
| **Croatia** | 24 | 5.5 | 10 | 12.8 | 533 |
| **Czech Republic** | 42 | 8.3 | 29.6 | 23.8 | 192 |
| **Estonia** | 9 | 1.3 | 26.4 | 14.7 | 619 |
| **Georgia** | 26 | – | 4.7 | – | – |
| **Hungary** | 62 | 41 | 12.5 | 21.9 | 283 |
| **Kazakhstan** | 14 | 9.9 | 7.6 | 9.4 | 888 |
| **Kyrgyz Republic** | 37 | 9.2 | 1.1 | 298.1 | 73248 |
| **Latvia** | 9 | 2.3 | 9.4 | 14.8 | 1755 |
| **Lithuania** | 16 | 2.9 | 12.2 | 10.8 | 554 |
| **Moldova** | 39 | 6.2 | 3.2 | 17.4 | 1394 |

| | | | | | |
|---|---|---|---|---|---|
| **Mongolia** | 65 | 9.7 | 1.3 | 16.6 | 1960 |
| **Poland** | 31 | 6.4 | 0.2 | 13.4 | 21612 |
| **Romania** | 23 | 12.6 | 9.8 | 8.9 | 393 |
| **Russia** | 25 | 9.6 | 9.5 | 3.7 | 155 |
| **Slovak Republic** | 41 | 11.9 | 38.3 | 20.5 | 131 |
| **Slovenia** | 21 | 8.7 | 1.4 | 12.4 | 4210 |
| **Tajikistan** | 24 | 0.1 | 1.9 | – | – |
| **Turkmenistan** | 18 | 10.6 | 34.8 | – | – |
| **Ukraine** | 18 | 6.1 | 4.8 | 4.5 | 519 |
| **Uzbekistan** | 9 | 8.1 | 3.9 | – | – |
| **Vietnam** | 123 | 3.5 | 14.5 | 5.7 | 32 |
| | | **Latin America** | | | |
| **Argentina** | 31 | 44.2 | 13 | 6.7 | 166 |
| **Brazil** | 26 | 41.1 | 19.8 | 8.0 | 155 |
| **Chile** | 48 | 32.3 | 25.5 | 20.9 | 171 |
| **Mexico** | 44 | 35.4 | 19.1 | 5.8 | 69 |
| **Peru** | 43 | 35.4 | 22.1 | 18.0 | 190 |
| **Venezuela** | 51 | 16.8 | 8.2 | 23.8 | 569 |
| | | **Asia** | | | |
| **India** | 22 | 24.1 | 7.5 | 7.0 | 424 |
| **Indonesia** | 64 | 36.8 | 25 | 8.6 | 54 |
| **Malaysia** | 52 | 8.2 | 27.8 | 28.1 | 194 |
| **Pakistan** | 39 | 27.4 | 9.4 | 2.0 | 55 |
| **Philippines** | 51 | 13.7 | 19.3 | 14.0 | 142 |
| **Thailand** | 56 | 11.5 | 41.4 | 20.9 | 90 |

SOURCE: World Bank (1998).

TABLE 3.2

**Ratio of Actual Exchange Rate of National Currencies in US$ to PPP for Selected Countries in 1993**

(In percentages; figures in brackets for 1996)

| *Countries/regions* | *Ratio, %* | | *Countries/regions* | *Ratio, %* | |
|---|---|---|---|---|---|
| OECD* | 116 | | Transition economies* | 81 | |
| – Germany | 126 | (133) | – Eastern Europe* | 54 | |
| – Japan | 165 | (158) | – Bulgaria | 30 | (25) |
| – U.S. | 100 | (100) | – Croatia | 65 | (94) |
| – Portugal | 73 | (77) | – Czech Republic | 36 | (48) |
| Developing countries* | 44 | | – Hungary | 62 | (63) |
| – Asia* | 36 | | – Poland | 48 | (59) |
| – India | 24 | (23) | – Romania | 31 | (34) |
| – Indonesia | 30 | (33) | – Slovak Republic | 37 | (47) |
| – Korea | 72 | (81) | – Slovenia | 69 | (78) |
| – Malaysia | | (44) | – USSR* | 91 | |
| – Philippines | 35 | (34) | – Armenia | | (20) |
| – Thailand | 43 | (45) | – Azerbaijan | | (32) |
| – Turkey | 54 | (48) | – Belarus | 8 | (30) |

| | | | | | |
|---|---|---|---|---|---|
| – Latin America* | 46 | | – Estonia | 29 | (64) |
| – Argentina | | (90) | – Georgia | | (29)** |
| – Brazil | | (70) | – Kazakhstan | | (39) |
| – Chile | | (43) | – Kyrgyz Republic | | (19) |
| – Mexico | 58 | (45) | – Latvia | 27 | (50) |
| – Peru | | (56) | – Lithuania | 19 | (47) |
| – Venezuela | | (36) | – Moldova | 14 | (28) |
| – Middle East* | 83 | | – RUSSIA | 26 | (70) |
| – Kuwait | | (67) | – Tajikistan | | (3) |
| – Saudi Arabia | | (68) | – Turkmenistan | | (45) |
| – United Arab Emirates | | (100) | – Ukraine | 19 | (39) |
| – Africa* | 37 | | – Uzbekistan | | (22) |
| – Ethiopia | | (20) | China | 22 | (20) |
| – Mozambique | | (17) | Mongolia | | (21) |
| – Nigeria | 36 | (90) | Vietnam | | (20) |

*1990. ** 1995.

SOURCE: UN International Comparison Program (Russian Statistical Yearbook 1997. Moscow, Goskomstat 1997, p.698; Finansoviye Izvestiya, 10 November 1995); World Bank, 1998; Transition Report 1997.

the exchange rate as compared to PPP, on the one hand, and the level of development (GDP per capita) and the ratio of reserves to exports, on the other. To put it differently, there are generally two major reasons for relatively undervalued exchange rates: (1) the generally lower level of development, imposing the burden on the balance of payments in the form of the capital flight and debt service payments (non-policy factor) and (2) the governments/central banks conscious policy to underprice the exchange rate in order to use it as an instrument of export-oriented growth (policy factor).

If these considerations apply equally to the developing and transition economies, it means that growth with macroeconomic stability is best secured by targeting an equilibrium real exchange rate level that is substantially below the PPP rate. This implies that a continuous appreciation of the real exchange rate is only an invitation for trouble and would sooner or later result in the currency crisis.

## Roots of the Currency Crises in Transition Economies

One view is that the transition economies were innocent victims of the volatile movements of capital in the global economy and had been swept into the Asian contagion. This view is not supported by the evidence. First, Bulgaria and Romania experienced their currency crises in 1996, before the first wave of the Asian crisis broke out in July 1997. Second, as we are going to show by examining more closely the Russian case, the room for the real appreciation of the national currencies in transition economies was limited and had been exceeded, and the onset of these crises were only a matter of time.

The specifics of the exchange rate policy in transition economies are determined, among other factors, by the challenge of macroeconomic stabilization, which policy makers faced in most post-communist countries after the deregulation of prices. Economists and policy makers have disagreed on what kind of exchange rate policy is best for economies in transition. Some have stressed the importance of maintaining a stable nominal exchange rate by fixing it and using it as a nominal anchor to fight inflation — an approach that is called an exchange rate based price stabilization (Bofinger, Flassbeck, and Hoffmann 1997). Others emphasize the importance of keeping the real exchange stable (which implies continual nominal devaluations, if inflation is higher than elsewhere) — to ensure that the actual rate is substantially below the PPP rate — in order to stimulate exports and growth.

Each approach has its own advantages. The first may prove to be useful for fighting high inflation quickly at the initial stages of macroeconomic stabilization. The second one may be better suited for overcoming transformational recession and promoting economic recovery by facilitating the transfer of resources from domestic demand to exports, which is a pressing need in all economies in transition.[13]

The conventional shock-therapy approach to macroeconomic stabilization recommends using the pegged exchange rate as a "nominal anchor" while pursuing an anti-inflationary policy (Sachs 1994, 1995; Åslund 1994). There is certainly merit in such an argument since a strong currency keeps the cost of imports down; by competing with local goods, imported goods help to hold down inflation. Such a pattern did in fact occur in many EE and FSU countries, including Russia in 1995–98.

Other countries in the region introduced currency boards (Estonia, Lithuania, Bulgaria, Bosnia and Herzegovina) and were initially successful in fighting inflation and promoting growth. Still other post-communist states exercised fixed nominal exchange rate regimes (Czech Republic, Hungary, Poland, Slovakia) with a fair degree of success as well.

However, there have been many precedents most especially in Latin America where the exchange-rate based stabilization had been maintained too long and caused the same kind of distortions now evident in the EE and FSU countries; a recent case is that of Mexico before its crisis in 1994, where it appears that authorities might have targeted too low an inflation rate (Griffith-Jones 1997). If Mexican authorities accepted moderate inflation, the rate of real exchange appreciation would have been more modest and the lending boom that ultimately triggered the Mexican crisis might not have been as large.

The inconsistency of the macroeconomic policy objectives in transition economies was discussed by Nuti (1996) well before the crises broke out. He stressed the:

> underlying widespread disequilibrium in the exchange rate regimes of many post-communist countries, primarily due to attempts at targeting simultaneously inconsistent values of three variables: i) nominal monetary aggregates to be held down to control inflation; ii) real interest rates to be kept significantly positive in order to encourage savings, thus also contributing to holding down inflation; iii) real exchange rates, whose increase is to be held down in order not to lose competitiveness. But something has to give: in an open economy with free trade and capital movements there is no way than one of these variables can be set by national authorities.

However, as already mentioned, virtually all transition economies experienced an appreciation of the real exchange rate since the start of the transition. Domestic inflation has uniformly been higher than external inflation and the nominal exchange rate did not adjust sufficiently to reflect the inflation differential. This pattern undermined the competitiveness of exporters, worsened the current account, and forced monetary authorities to maintain high interest rates (to slow down the capital flight and attract new foreign financing) at a time when exactly the opposite was needed. At the present time, even in those countries which avoided the currency crisis, the real appreciation of the exchange rate has become a major policy concern.

In countries which relied on currency board arrangements longer than others (Estonia — since June 1992 and Lithuania since October 1994), domestic prices also continued to increase despite the stability of the nominal exchange rate that is inherent in such an arrangement. The resulting real appreciation of the currencies of these countries have been accompanied by an increase of the current account deficit to over 10 per cent of GDP in 1998; moreover, domestic financing in these economies now totally depends on the inflow of foreign capital. As of this writing, both countries have managed to withstand the Asian crisis and the Russian crisis, but their growth rates in 1998 fell significantly and the prospects for growth 1999 are not encouraging.

In the wake of the Russian economic crisis, it appears that the overvaluation of the national currencies of the transition economies in EE and FSU is hindering economic growth and creating the threat of the currency crises. There seems to be a growing recognition that the exchange rate may be far too important to use only for fighting inflation. Even in the case of those transition economies that have already achieved macroeconomic stability, such as Poland and the Czech Republic, the issue is of even greater importance since these are now preoccupied with attaining economic growth. The policy of keeping the *real* exchange rate stable, instead of pegging the *nominal* rate, has increased its appeal to policy makers, after the currency crises of 1996–98.

The evidence suggests that among the transition economies, those that maintained stable real exchange rates for quite a time are presently doing no worse than others. Countries (Albania, Slovenia, Croatia, FYR Macedonia) that pursued the alternative approach of a "money-based" stabilization and relied more heavily on controlling increases in money supply and less on keeping the nominal exchange rates fixed for fighting inflation have been just as successful in stabilizing their economies as those that succeeded through exchange rate based stabilization (Zettermeyer and Citrin 1995). With an appropriate monetary policy (which included the partial sterilization of increases in the money supply caused by the foreign exchange reserves build up), the inflationary pressure was dealt with.

While the operational technicalities of managing an undervalued exchange rate need not be discussed here, it may be appropriate to mention that such a policy has some important practical advantages. Unlike other measures to promote growth, undervaluing the exchange rate may provoke less political resistance. The policy favours the interests of a broad range of powerful industrial groups (creating a stimulus for the export-oriented sector, as well as providing protection from import competition for industries dependent primarily on the domestic market). The costs of a policy of an undervalued exchange rate such as the restrictions on consumption are to be paid by unorganized and politically less influential consumers. In addition, an undervalued exchange rate policy can be superior to trade protectionism (which relies for its efficacy in the creation of some scope for bureaucratic discretion in the selection of priority industries and enterprises)[14] because it minimizes the potential for corruption: it provides benefits to all exporters.

# 4
# RUSSIA'S 1998 FINANCIAL COLLAPSE

Perhaps the most spectacular of all currency crises among the transition economies was the one that which broke out in Russia in August 1998. In a matter of days, the rouble that had remained relatively stable during the preceding 3 years lost over 60 per cent of its value (Figure 3.1); prices increased by 50 per cent within 2 months after the crisis, as compared to the less than 1 per cent monthly inflation before the crisis. (See Figures 4.1 and 4.2.) Annual real output fell by about 6 per cent in 1998 after registering a small increase of 0.6 per cent in 1997 for the first time since 1989 and is expected to fall by a similar amount in 1999 (Figure 4.3).

## The Almost Successful Stabilization Effort

What is worse, the financial collapse in Russia marked the failure of the government programme of macroeconomic stabilization that had been pursued for over 3 years with a fair degree of success. After experiencing high inflation of several hundred and more per cent a year during the period immediately following the deregulation of prices on 2 January 1992, Russia finally opted for the programme of the exchange rate based stabilization. In mid-1995, the Central Bank of Russia (CBR) after accumulating foreign exchange reserves and achieving a degree of stability for the rouble in the first half of 1995, introduced a crawling peg system — an

FIGURE 4.1
**Annual Inflation Rates, Russia, 1990–99**
(December-to-December rates)

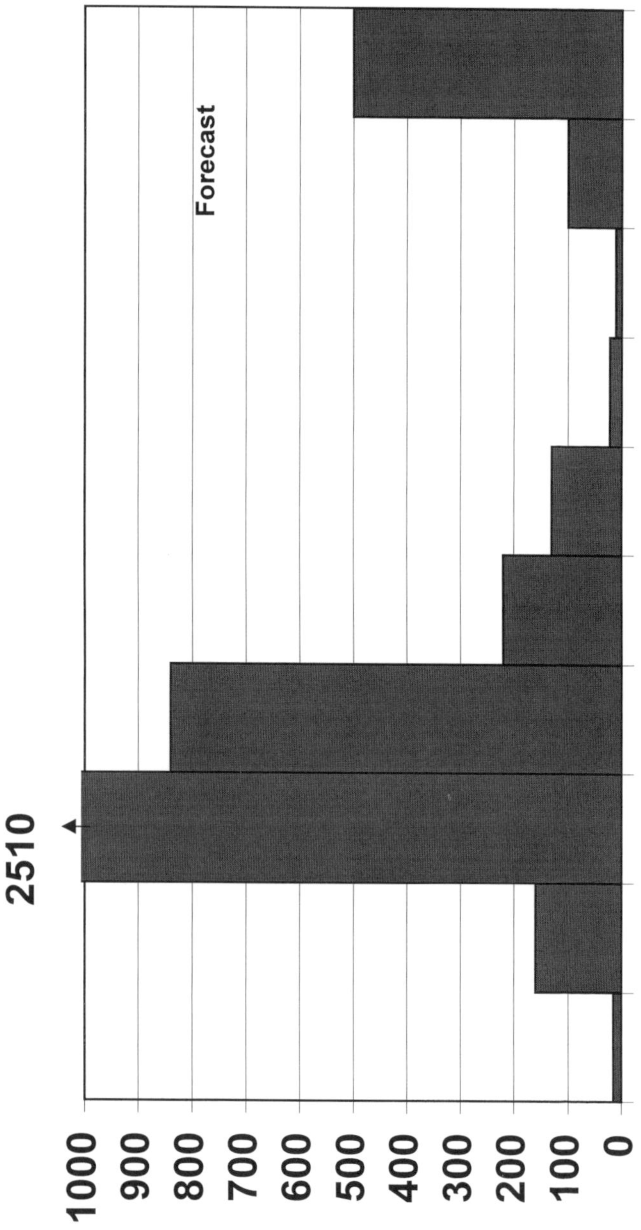


SOURCE: Goskomstat.

FIGURE 4.2
**Monthly Inflation Rates, Russia, Jan 98–Nov 98**

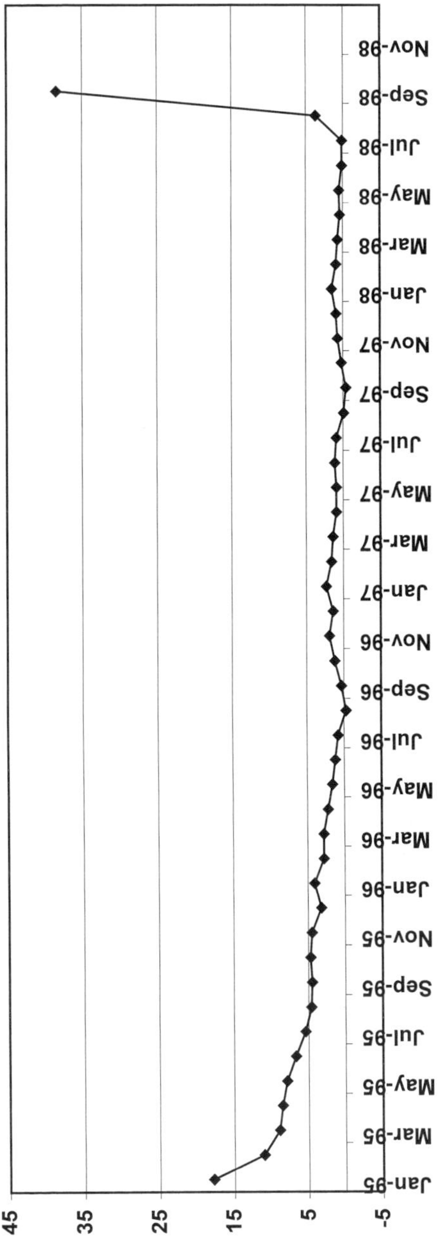


SOURCE: Goskomstat.

FIGURE 4.3
**Russia's GDP Growth Rates, 1990–99**
(Percentages)

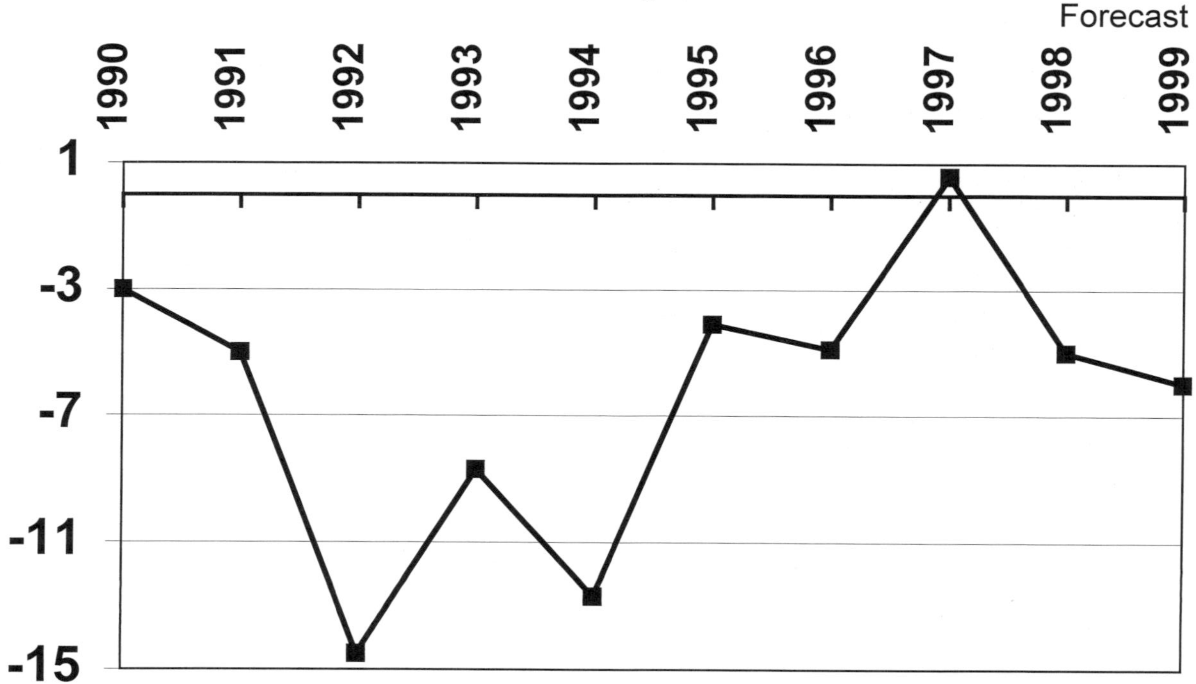


SOURCE: Goskomstat.

FIGURE 4.5
**Russian Government Revenues and Expenditure**
(Percentage of GDP)

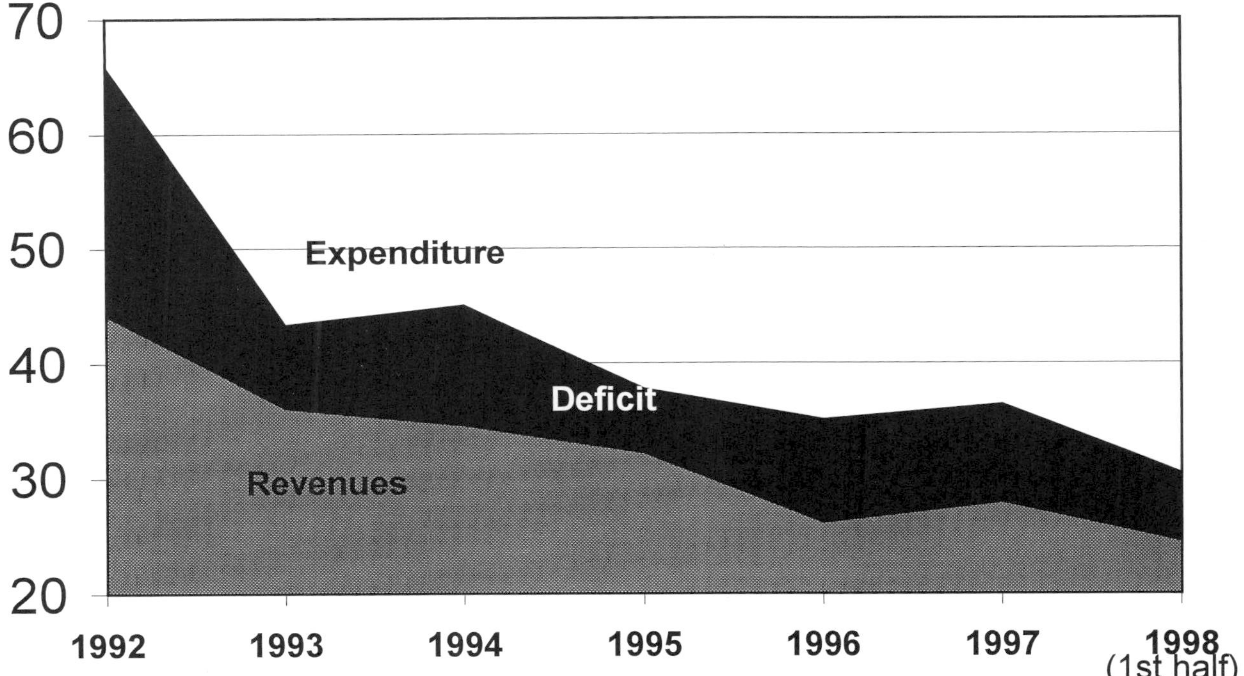


SOURCE: EBRD, 1996, 1997, 1998.

## Dutch Disease and the Perils of Currency Overvaluation

As a result, the "Dutch disease" enveloped Russia after 1995 and the symptoms were quite evident. The exchange rate of the rouble approached some 70 per cent of the PPP and stayed at this level until the crisis (Table 3.2); this level is much higher than the 20 to 50 per cent that we had identified as suitable for most developing and transition economies. The previously high export growth rates slowed down substantially (from 20 per cent in 1995 to 8 per cent in 1996 — for total exports, and from 25 per cent to 9 per cent respectively — for exports to non-CIS states).[15] In 1997 the growth rate of total exports turned negative for the first time since 1992. Needless to say, it was Russia's already weak manufactured exports industries that was most affected by the appreciation of real exchange rate. The profitability of these industries was also being squeezed by high Russian internal costs, which had risen with inflation. In 1996, among the economies in transition, Russia (together with Slovenia, by far the richest transition country, experiencing recovery from 1993) had the smallest gap between domestic and international prices (Table 4.1).[16]

Falling oil prices in the world market in 1997–98 added insult to injury. Export growth rates turned even more negative in the first half of 1998, which together with still rising imports virtually wiped out the trade surplus. In better times, such as in 1996, the trade surplus had amounted to $20 billion (Figure 4.6). The current account balance turned negative in the first half of 1998 (Figure 4.7). Given the need to service the external debt and the continuation of the capital flight (which is partly captured in the "errors and omissions" in the balance of payments statistics in Fugure 4.7), the switch from positive to negative balances in the current account was a sure recipe for disaster. Based on an

TABLE 4.1

**Ratio of the Actual Exchange Rate to the PPP Rate of the Dollar for Selected Economies in Transition**

(Range of monthly averages)

| *Country/Year* | *1990* | *1991* | *1992* | *1993* | *1994* | *1995* | *1996* | *1997* | *1998* |
|---|---|---|---|---|---|---|---|---|---|
| Slovenia | 0.9–1.4 | 1.0–1.7 | 1.4–1.6 | 1.4–1.6 | 1.3–1.6 | 1.1–1.3 | 1.3–1.3 | 1.4–1.5 | 1.4–1.5 |
| Hungary | 1.9–2.4 | 1.9–2.0 | 1.7–1.8 | 1.6–1.8 | 1.6–1.8 | 1.5–1.6 | 1.7–1.8 | 1.6–1.8 | 1.7–1.7 |
| Poland | 2.1–3.9 | 1.6–1.9 | 1.8–2.0 | 1.8–2.0 | 2.1–2.3 | 1.8–2.0 | 1.8–1.8 | 1.8–2.1 | 1.9–1.9 |
| Czech Republic | 2.5–3.8 | 3.5–3.1 | 2.7–3.1 | 2.5–2.6 | 2.2–2.5 | 2.0–2.2 | 1.9–2.0 | 2.0–2.3 | 2.0–2.3 |
| Slovak Republic | 2.9–3.9 | 3.0–3.6 | 2.9–3.0 | 2.6–2.8 | 2.4–2.7 | 2.1–2.3 | 2.1–2.2 | 2.3–2.4 | 2.3–2.6 |
| Lithuania | – | – | – | – | 2.4–3.2 | 1.8–2.3 | 1.7–1.8 | 1.5–1.6 | – |
| Romania | 1.8–2.6 | 1.6–5.0 | 2.8–4.2 | 2.2–3.1 | 2.1–2.6 | 2.1–2.5 | 2.4–2.6 | 2.0–3.3 | 1.8–2.0 |
| Bulgaria | 3.3–5.1 | 2.9–10.9 | 3.0–4.7 | 2.3–2.8 | 2.3–3.1 | 1.8–2.2 | 1.9–2.8 | 1.7–3.2 | 1.5–1.8 |
| Ukraine | – | – | – | – | – | 1.8–2.5 | 1.3–1.7 | 1.3–1.4 | – |
| RUSSIA | – | 33.0–131.0 | 10.2–45.7 | 2.5–8.0 | 2.4–2.8 | 1.4–2.4 | 1.4–1.5 | 1.4–1.5 | 1.4–1.5 |

SOURCE: PlanEcon (Data for the second half of 1998 are forecasts for Slovenia, Czech Republic, Romania, Bulgaria, and Russia. For Slovakia, all 1998 data are forecasts; for Poland data for March–December 1998 are forecasts; for Ukraine data for the fall of 1997 are forecast; for Lithuania, all 1997 data are forecasts. For Hungary data are for January–March 1998 only).

FIGURE 4.6
**Russia's Foreign Trade, 1993–98**
(Billion dollars)

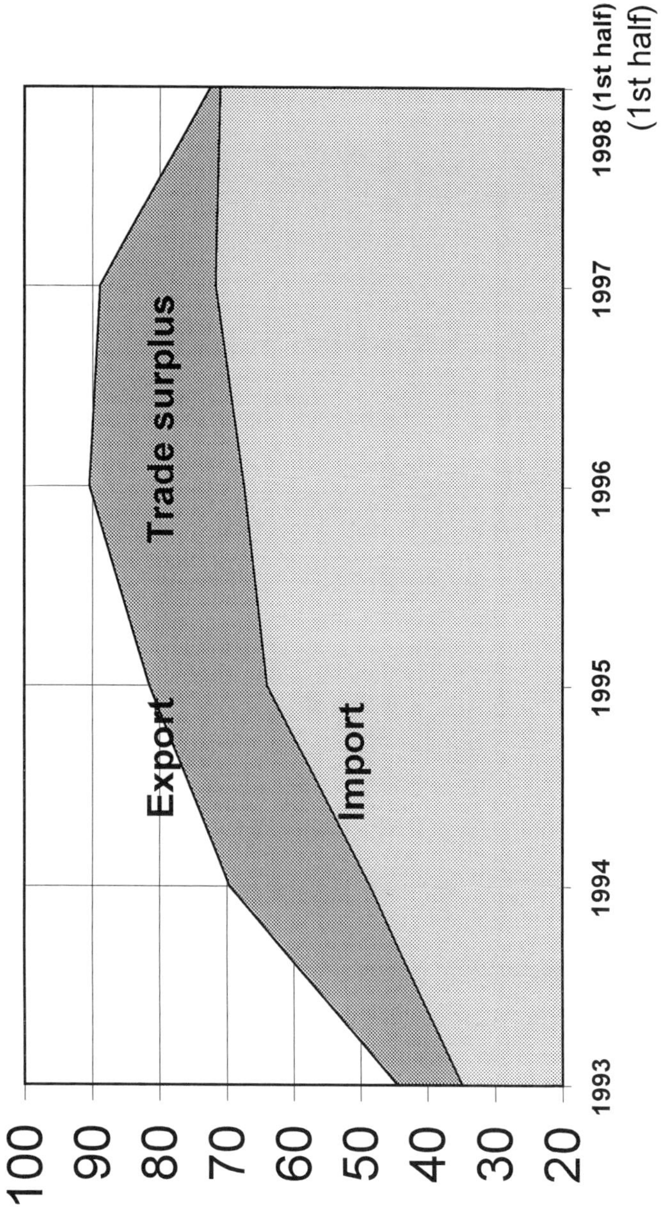


SOURCE: Goskomstat.

FIGURE 4.7
**Russia's Balance of Payments and Foreign Exchange Reserves***
(Billion dollars)

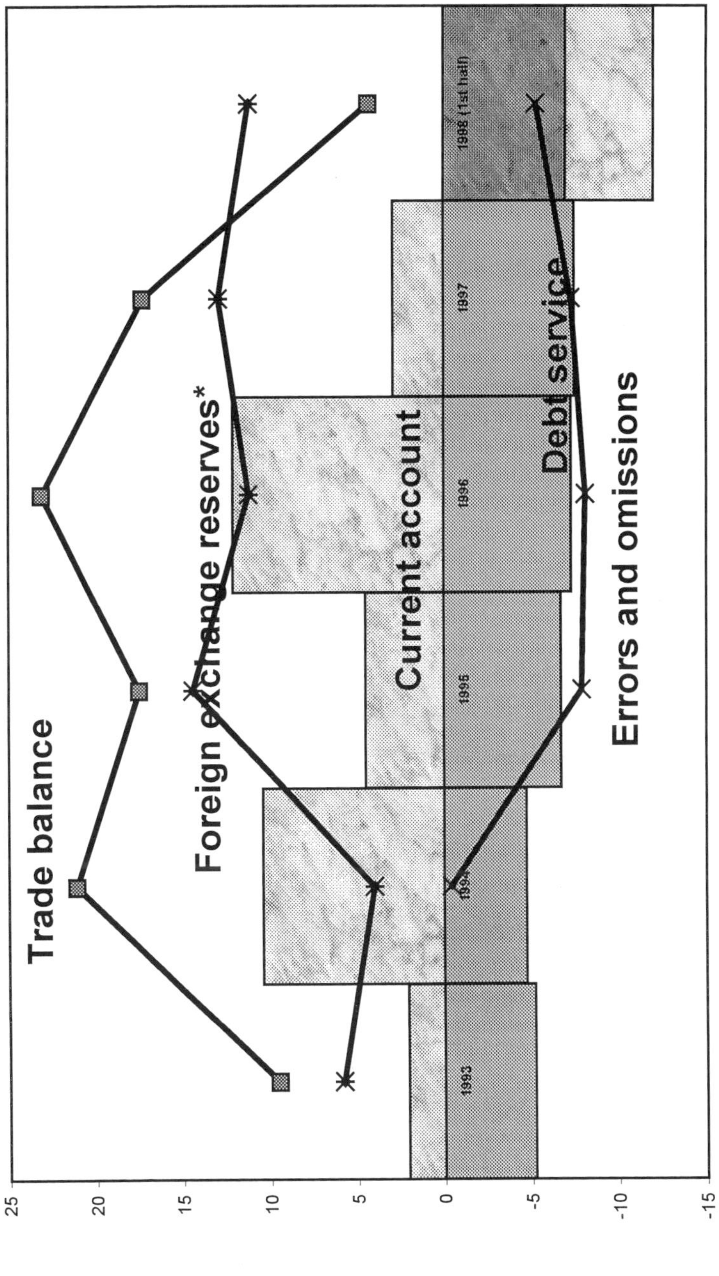


SOURCE: Goskomstat.
*Year end, excluding gold.

analysis of the structural features of Russian external trade, Desai (1997) emphasizes the critical role the real exchange rate plays in restraining imports.

Thus the overvaluation of the rouble by itself created a clear potential for the currency crisis and caused the outflow of capital from Russia. In fact, under the circumstances, the exchange rate became hardly sustainable in 1998 since there developed a new vulnerability of the rouble with respect to short-term capital flows. Since they were allowed by authorities in 1995, foreign investment into rouble-denominated government treasury bills quickly increased to nearly one third of $50 billion market for government treasury bills by 1997 (including investment into the GKO through "gray schemes", i.e. through resident intermediaries). From February 1998, the total amount of T-bills held by the non-residents started to exceed the value of the country's foreign exchange reserves (*Economist*, 23 May 1998). This also happened in Mexico when, beginning in June 1994, the value of dollar-denominated Treasury bills called *Tesobonos*, held by many mutual and pension funds in New York, exceeded total reserves (Griffith-Jones 1997).

Foreign investors also started to withdraw from the Russian stock market. They were estimated to control no less than 10 per cent of the shares in the booming Russian stock market whose capitalization surpassed $100 billion in the fall 1997. Since that time until mid-1998, in just about 9 months, the stock prices in dollar terms fell by about 90 per cent to the lowest level since 1994 (Figure 4.8). The decision of the CBR to expand slightly the width of the exchange rate band from the beginning of 1998 was a cosmetic measure and did not yield much room for the maneuver. The Central Bank had to increase the refinancing rate to 150 per cent in May 1998 to prevent capital from fleeing at a rate of about $0.5 billion a week at a time when

FIGURE 4.8

**Dollar Stock Prices Indices, 1992–98**

(Dec. 1993 = 100)

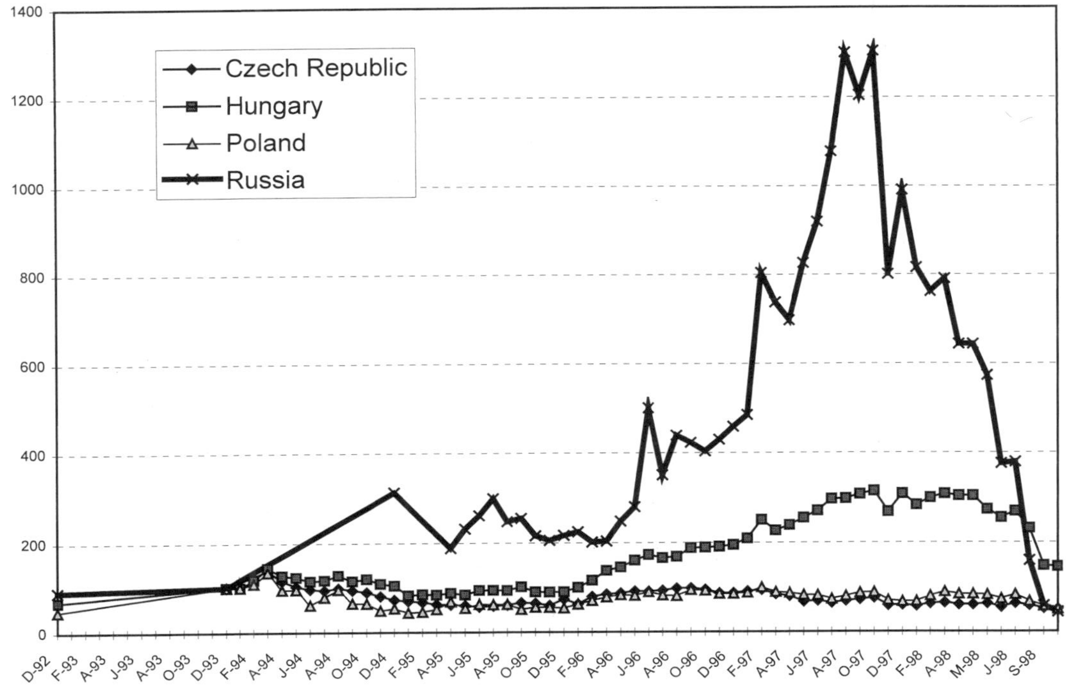


SOURCE: *Economist*. (For Russia in 1992–93, estimates of the Graduate School of International Business, Academy of National Economy).

foreign exchange reserves were at level of about $15 billion. Later the refinancing rate was lowered, but yields on government securities remained at a level of nearly 50 per cent in real terms and then again increased to over 100 per cent in August 1998.

The central bank and the government, however, played the "confidence game" up to the very last moment, negotiating a stand-by package with the IMF and clinging to the policy of strong rouble. This policy compelled the authorities to maintain scandalously high domestic interest rates. The high interest rate regime eliminated all prospects for economic recovery. In a sense, this was a policy designed to maintain consumption and imports, to avoid export-oriented restructuring and to continue to live beyond the economy's means through increasing dependence on foreign finance. The IMF finally provided the first installment ($4 billion) of the $20 billion dollar package that went directly to the CBR to replenish vanishing foreign exchange reserves, but even this did not calm the investors. Public officials' statements about the stability of the rouble, including that of President B. Yeltsin made three days before devaluation, had only the opposite effect, if any.

In retrospect, it is pretty obvious that the crisis was caused by the unrealistic and counterproductive attempts of the Russian government and CBR, as well as of IMF, to defend an unsustainably high exchange rate of the rouble. This is not an argument against the fixed exchange rate, but rather an argument against a currency peg at an unrealistically high level. There is a difference between a stable and a strong currency: whereas the former may be desirable in particular circumstances, the latter may prove to be an unaffordable luxury for economies in transition, like Russia, trying to overcome the transformational recession. It may well be therefore that the CBR and the government were right to establish a sort of a crawling peg for the rouble, but were wrong in choosing to peg it at a level that had a deleterious impact on the real sector. Having chosen such a level, it became increasingly difficult to devalue the rouble without risking an uncontrolled free fall in its value since an adjustment could very easily induce the collapse of confidence in the rouble.

By pegging the rouble at a weaker rate and continuing to build up foreign exchange reserves, the CBR could have killed more than two birds with one stone. First, Russian exports and trade surplus would have improved; second, domestic interest rates would have fallen and there would have been an additional stimulus for the "de-dollarization" of the Russian economy and for the inflow of foreign direct investment. A weaker rouble, to put it differently, could have been a device for maintaining higher saving rates without high interest rates, to create additional stimulus for production, investment and exports, while limiting consumption and imports. Keeping the rouble at a lower level would thus not only be a prudent policy to avoid a currency crisis, but also could have been an instrument of export-oriented strategy encouraging restructuring and growth.

We had strongly taken the position, along with some other economists, that before the crisis broke out, the rouble was overvalued. As the probability of a crisis increased, it also seemed prudent to forewarn that if the rouble was not devalued "from above" in advance of a crisis situation, it would likely get devalued "from below", in the form of a currency crisis, with much greater costs (Popov 1996 *a*, *b*, 1997, 1998 *b*, *c*).[17] In a sense, it was not too difficult to predict the Russian crisis and quite a number of scholars did so several months ahead of time. Even Jeffrey Sachs, previously a strong advocate of Russia's exchange rate based stabilization, spoke out publicly in favour of devaluation in June 1998 (*New York Times*, 4 June 1998).[18]

## The Completely Unnecessary Debt Default

What virtually no one predicted was the manner in which the Russian Government handled the financial consequences of the devaluation, that is by declaring a default on the domestic debt and on part of the international debt held by banks and companies. *The debt default was completely unnecessary.*

On 17 August 1998, Russia did not have a debt crisis, only a currency crisis, which was already being addressed by means of devaluing the rouble. As of that date, total Russian debt as a proportion of GDP amounted to less than 50 per cent. As Figure 4.9 suggests, the indebtedness of the Russian government in recent years was indeed growing, but not that significantly as compared to GDP (since GDP in dollar terms was growing rapidly due to the real appreciation of the rouble). In absolute terms the total government debt by mid-1998 had not even reached the conventionally considered danger threshold of 60 per cent of GDP.

True, government short term obligations — GKOs, rouble denominated, but held by non-residents, since early 1998, according to available estimates, exceeded total foreign exchange reserves. This indicated some obvious mismanagement, unheedful of the experience of Mexico in 1994 (Calvo and Mendoza 1996) and clearly contributed to the crisis. However, the absolute value of the outstanding short-term debt held by the foreigners was by no means substantial — only $15–20 billion, which represented only 10 per cent of total foreign debt. Even though the level of international reserves ($15 billion) would have been insufficient to cover the short-term obligations, it would still have been possible to continue to service the short-term

FIGURE 4.9
**Russian Government Debt, 1994–98**
(Percentage of GDP)

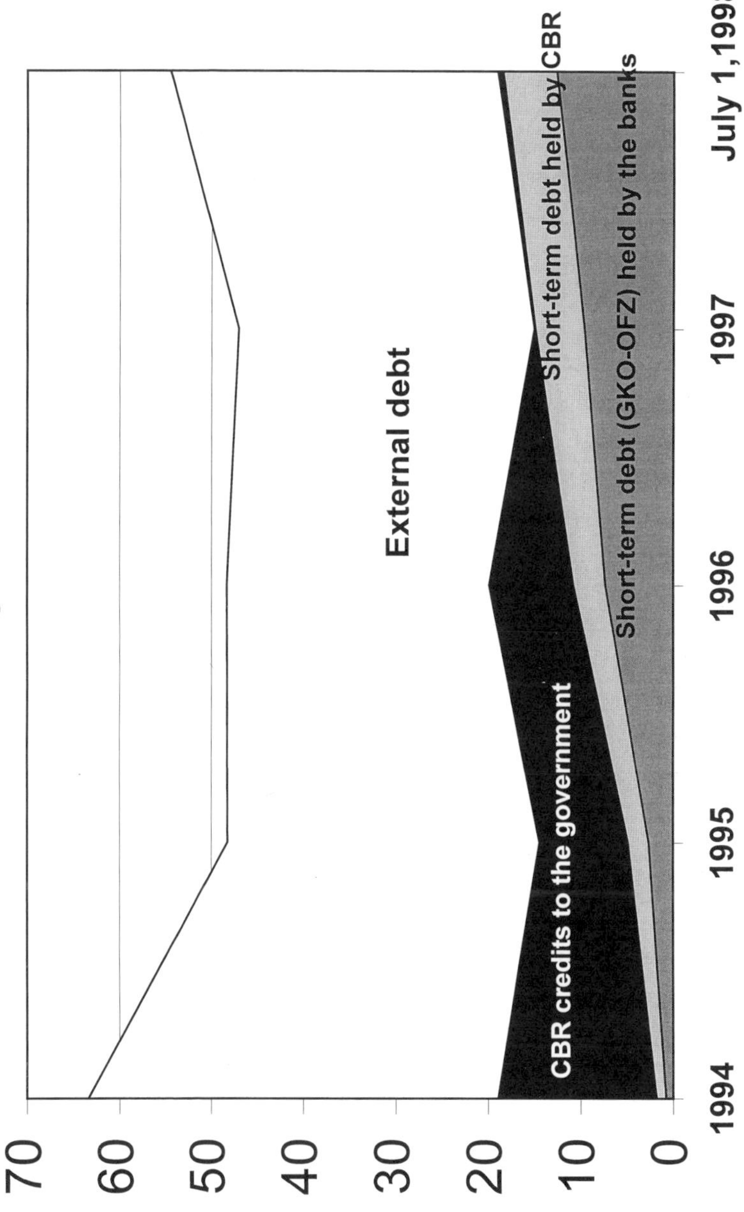


SOURCE: "Russian Economy". *The Month in Review*. No. 1 (1998). Bank of Finland, Institute for Economies in Transition; Goskomstat.

external debt after, say a 50 per cent devaluation.[19] In the first place, the short-term obligations were denominated in roubles; a 50 per cent devaluation would have implied a halving of the dollar requirements to service the debt. In the second place, an orderly handling of the debt would have kept IMF credits in place and these could be used for servicing the short-term debt.

The mistrust on the part of investors beginning in the first half of 1998 was associated first and foremost with the low credibility of the government policy to defend the rouble at all costs; the ability of the government to service its debt was not really put into question. This can be inferred from the costs of borrowing before the crisis. The difference between the rates at which the Russian Government borrowed abroad in hard currency (returns on Eurobonds were around 15 per cent) and the rates offered to the prime borrowers (7 per cent) was much lower than the gap between returns on rouble denominated bonds (about 100 per cent in real terms) and Eurobonds (15 per cent). Because the first gap is an indicator of the country risk (i.e., the risk associated with the default by the government of this particular country), whereas the second one reflects the currency risk (i.e., the risk associated with the possibility of a devaluation), it is clear that the anticipation of the market at that time was that of devaluation, but not of debt default.

Unfortunately, the default was not the only element of mismanagement in dealing with the crisis. Shortly after the default, the CBR provoked, by its clumsy actions, a run on the banks and a banking crisis. Banks had already been badly hurt by the devaluation; these costs could be viewed as inevitable and unavoidable for all parties. They were also hurt by the debt default, because they held a considerable portion of their assets in short-term government securities and also because they lost access to external financing after the government imposed a 90-day moratorium on servicing the banks' own external debts. To make matters worse, the CBR in early September introduced a scheme meant to guarantee personal deposits in the commercial banks but which effectively imposed losses on the depositors, especially for the holders of dollar accounts at private banks.

Under the scheme, the CBR sought to extend the guarantees on deposits that had previously been available only in state-owned *Sberbank* (Savings Bank)[20] to personal deposits at commercial banks. To qualify for such guarantees, the CBR required depositors to move their deposits to *Sberbank*, a method that by itself would have provoked withdrawals. Moreover, the CBR promised to allow withdrawals into cash only after 2 months and only in part (dollar deposits, for instance, were supposed to be converted into roubles at a 1 September rate of 9.33 roubles per dollar, at a time when the market rate of the dollar was already about 2 times higher). The run at the banks that naturally followed contributed to the developing paralysis of the banking system. In September 1998, banks were hardly processing any payments and businesses started to carry out their transactions purely in cash, barter and cash substitutes.

## Alternative Explanations for the Crisis

The most popular alternative explanations for the Russian crisis are those associated in one way or another with the crony and criminal nature of the Russian capitalism. The government is accused of playing into the interests of "oligarchs", heads of large financial-industrial groups in the Russian economy, that have effectively "privatized" the state and care only about enriching themselves in the short run. The assumption basically is that everything is so rotten in Russia that there is no way the exchange rate can be stable.

One variation of these views is that the construction of the government debt pyramid was doomed to collapse and eventually collapsed. It is pointed out that the returns on the short-term government bonds (GKOs) were scandalously high, many times higher than in the real sector, and that such a policy was driving away resources from the real sector into purely financial speculation in the market for government debt and the stock market (Nekipelov 1998). Financial prosperity, not based on the foundations of the healthy real economy, could not continue for long and finally came to an end in the form of the crisis.

Another variation is that funds obtained by the state through domestic and external borrowing were mishandled, if not embezzled or stolen and that overall the inefficient and corrupt system of the public administration could not ensure any kind of macroeconomic stabilization, be it exchange rate-based of money-based. Oligarchs were not thinking long-term anyway and are unable to agree on measures to increase the tax revenues of the state, to slow down capital flight and to control the indebtedness, since, as Paul Krugman puts it, 'there is no honour among the thieves" (10 Sept. 1998).

These explanations, however, to a large extent miss the point. There is hardly any doubt that Russian state institutions were degrading in recent years and that the weakening of the state institutions is the main *long-term* factor explaining the poor performance of the Russian economy (and other economies in the Commonwealth of Independent States) as compared to China and Vietnam with strong authoritarian institutions, on the one hand, and Central European countries with strong democratic institutions, on the other. As a matter of fact, a recent research study comparing 28 transition economies, including those of China and Vietnam, suggests that it is not the speed of liberalisation, which should be held responsible for differing performance, but the institutional capacity of the state — the factor that was overlooked by both schools of thought in transition economics — by shock therapists and by gradualists (Popov 1999).

In most FSU and Balkan countries the collapse of the institutions is observable in the dramatic increase of the share of the shadow economy; in the decline of government revenues as a proportion of GDP; in the inability of the state to deliver basic public goods and appropriate regulatory framework; in the accumulation of tax, trade, wage and bank arrears; in the demonetization, "dollarization" and "barterization" of the economy, as measured by high and growing money velocity, in the decline of bank financing as a proportion of GDP; in poor enforcement of property rights, bankruptcies, contracts and law and order in general; and in increased crime rates; etc. Most of the above-mentioned phenomena may be measured quantitatively and the comparison indicates the remarkable result that China and Vietnam are closer in terms of these indicators to more successful Eastern European transition countries than to CIS. (See Figure 4.10.)

In Russia, the disintegration of the state institutions was perhaps most striking. Although the government should be credited for being able to cut government expenditure in line with the fall in revenues (Figure 4.5), the sharp reduction of the share of government revenues in GDP was by itself obviously a sign of institutional degradation. Besides, the reduction of the government expenditure occurred in the worst possible way: it proceeded chaotically, without any coherent plan and did not involve the reassessment of government commitments. Instead of shutting down completely some government programmes and concentrating limited resources on those left standing with the aim to raise their efficiency, the government kept all programmes half-alive, half-financed, and barely working.

FIGURE 4.10
**Government Expenditure, 1985–96**
(Percentage of GDP)

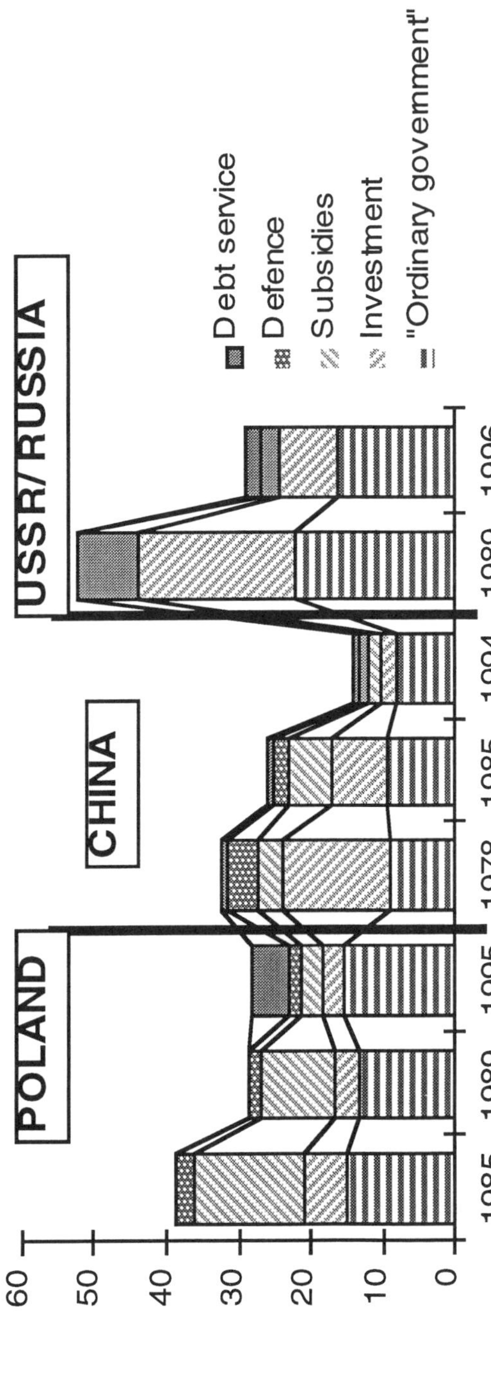

The poor administration of shrinking public funds turned into a major problem. As a result, excessively wide social responsibilities became financially unsustainable, and there emerged a gap between the obligations of the state and its ability to deliver what it promised.

There developed a slow decay of public education, health care, infrastructure, law and order institutions, fundamental research and development (R&D), and so on. Virtually all services provided by the government, from collecting custom duties to regulating street traffic, became the symbol of notorious economic inefficiency. These numerous cases of government failures further undermined the credibility of the state. Many government activities in providing public goods and social transfers were slowly dying and were replaced by private and semi-private businesses, which, of course, were not able to provide public goods with the same efficiency as the state.

In the former Soviet Union, not only were government regulations pervasive, but also the financial power of the state was roughly the same as in other European countries. This allowed the state to provide the bulk of public goods and extensive social transfers. In the post communist Russia (and other CIS countries) the state found itself deprived of former vast resources and powers. On the one hand, it turned out that government regulatory activities have only limited efficiency due to difficulties in enforcing regulations since the authoritarian regime was replaced by the weak democratic one (in contrast to Central Europe, where strong democratic regimes emerged). On the other hand, government revenues plummeted after the centrally planned economy was dismantled, falling below 30 per cent of GDP (including off-budget funds) in 1997. While the size of the government revenues as a proportion of GDP still exceeded those of East Asian countries on average, the value of the resources were much less than needed to finance government commitments. These commitments are still very large in the areas of agricultural and housing subsidies, in mostly free education and health care, and the universal pay-as-you-go system of social insurance.

Nevertheless, even though the institutional weakness is the single most important *long-term* factor that contributed to the extreme magnitude of the Russian recession, it is not linked directly with the collapse of the rouble and the failure of macroeconomic stabilization programme. As we argued earlier, the debt levels of the Russian Government and Russian companies were very modest by the international standards: even if the borrowed funds were embezzled, this could not and did not lead to the debt and currency crises, since the critical point of really excessive indebtedness had yet to be reached by at least several years. No less important, there was no major change with respect to "cronyness", corruption and institutional weaknesses in recent years (except, perhaps in some stabilization), so appeals to the criminal nature of Russian capitalism cannot explain the onset of the crisis.

Finally, the goal of maintaining the appropriate (not overvalued) exchange rate was perhaps the least politicized issue of the government economic policy: by keeping the rouble low through carrying out timely and gradual devaluation, the government and the CBR were not risking any opposition either from industrial lobbies, or from the oligarchs. While there are reasons to believe that macroeconomic stabilization in Russia did not materialize in 1992–94 because of the lack of consensus among powerful industrial lobbies on how to finance cuts in government expenditure (Popov 1996 *a*, *b*), there is no evidence whatsoever that a subsequent low rouble strategy in 1995–98 was not sustainable because of political considerations.

## Possible Options for 1999

Given that previous mistakes were made, i.e., that the rouble was not devalued early enough, the best way to deal with the crisis would have been just devaluation - but without any debt defaults and moratoria. This still remains the best of all possible options: to revoke the decisions on default (the moratorium expired in mid-November 1998 and the banks are now negotiating the restructuring of their debts with the creditors), but to leave the devalued floating rate of the rouble in place. Such an approach would restore confidence of the international investors: with the new devalued rate of the rouble and with the guarantees against new default, Russian assets would become a bargain and capital inflows should gradually resume. The repayment of about $6 billion — the new (after devaluation) dollar value of the rouble denominated treasury bills (GKOs) held by non-residents — is a small price to pay to restore international financing. The probability of this option, however, is close to zero, since the government by the end of 1998 was heading towards the restructuring of the debt and reached a preliminary agreement with the creditors in November 1998. The government approach involves payments of only 10 per cent of the debt in cash and the conversion of the rest of the debt into bonds with longer maturity.

The other option, which was discussed for a time in early September 1998 (after V. Chernomyrdyn succeeded S. Kiriyenko as an acting prime minister and before Y. Primakov took charge) is the introduction of the currency board. The idea is not new,[21] but has serious theoretical and practical shortcomings.

The theoretical objection is the possible deflationary impact of the currency board because it requires the full (or nearly full) backing of the money supply by foreign exchange reserves. Under such conditions, any outflow of capital inevitably results in the reduction of the money supply leading to a deflationary shock and provokes the reduction of output. At the end of the day, the question of the efficiency of the currency board arrangement for a particular country boils down to the empirical question, whether there is enough price flexibility to ensure that the deflationary shocks would not affect the real sectors. For small open economies, where domestic prices already depend heavily on world market prices (Hong Kong, Estonia, Lithuania, Bulgaria, Bosnia) the answer may be positive. For medium size countries (such as Argentina), there is still not enough evidence, not to speak about larger countries like Russia. Besides, there is evidence that the ability of the authorities to address banking problems through providing lender of last resort support weakens considerably with the introduction of the currency board, which thus makes it risky for countries with vulnerable banking systems (Santiprabhob 1997).

The practical objection to the currency board plan for Russia is even more persuasive. It is generally recognized (Hanke, Jonung and Schuler 1993) that the necessary precondition for the successful introduction of the currency board is the credibility of the government and of its ability to eliminate the budget deficit. And it is also generally accepted that the current Russian Government in this respect is among the least credible in the world.

In one way or another, the new Primakov government that took office in September 1998, made it clear that the currency board option is no longer being considered. Thus, at the time of writing (January 1999) Russia is left basically with two options for 1999, which depend crucially on the ability of the government to contain the expansion of the growing budget deficit.

The favourable option — soft landing — requires that the federal government budget deficit in 1999 would be limited to 1–2 per cent of GDP at most, and the expansion of the money supply and hence inflation would be limited to 20–40 per cent. The other option is that the deficit would amount to 5–10 per cent of GDP, which, in the absence of the opportunities to borrow domestically and abroad, is likely to produce inflation of several hundred per cent. This latter option is certainly less favourable, but unfortunately more probable: unless the government initiates a draconian programme of budget cuts, chances to contain the deficit look very slim.

The unexpected consequence of the crisis was the sharp reduction of government revenues. Businesses and regional governments responded to the financial turmoil and growing payment difficulties by withholding tax payments to the federal government. Federal budget revenues fell from 18 billion roubles in July 1998, before the crisis, to 11.2 billion in August, to 9.3 billion in September and 13 billion in October. Since prices over the period (August–October) increased 1.5 times, government revenues in real terms fell by about 2 times. Government expenditure before the crisis normally stood at a level of 30 billion roubles per month, including about 10 billion devoted to servicing the short-term debt.

In the last two months of 1998, the federal government faced the dilemma of either cutting expenditure to half its previous level in real terms or financing a deficit of nearly 10 per cent of GDP by money printing (since after the debt default external sources of financing had disappeared). Once again, the government responded to the challenge in an unpredictable way: instead of suggesting budget cuts, it offered a programme of tax reduction (the profit tax, for instance, is to be reduced from 35 to 30 per cent and the value-added tax from 20 to 15 per cent), which reinforced the fears of impending high inflation.

# 5
# THE CURRENCY CRISES IN EAST ASIA

The most visible evidence of the economic crisis in East Asia has been the collapses of the international value of the regional currencies after July 1997. Before then, these values had been stable, if not modestly appreciating.

Apart from the countries (Thailand, Indonesia and Korea) that had sought assistance from the IMF to defend their currencies, the economies of Hong Kong, the Philippines, Singapore, Taiwan have seen their currencies depreciate by at least 15 per cent; three other Asia-Pacific economics Australia, New Zealand, and Canada have suffered a similar fate. The Japanese yen, the only global currency in the region, also endured a fall in its dollar value by as much as 35 per cent in the first half of 1998 before recovering in September 1998, after the start of the Russian crisis. The renminbi, the currency of the People's Republic of China, has been seen to be under attack since the beginning of 1998 and there are many public predictions of its impending devaluation. It is natural to ask the question: did overvaluation of East Asian currencies cause their crises, as was the case of the transition economies?

## The Overvaluation/Competitiveness Explanation

We have suggested that in the case of the transition economies, the loss of competitiveness due to currency overvaluation was the key factor. Currency overvaluation is a real sector explanation, most easily understood using considerations of international trade. According to this view, by 1997, the export-oriented East Asian economies had lost a significant portion their international competitiveness, especially with respect to China but also against new entrants in world markets such as India and Vietnam.

Inflation rates had been modest before the crisis (and continue, to the surprise of many, to be modest, after the extreme devaluations).[22] Moreover, nominal exchange rates of the East Asian currencies had not fluctuated violently in the early 1990s. It would have to be the case that export-competitiveness has been lost through appreciations in the "real effective exchange rate". The real effective exchange rate is an indicator of the real world price of a country's exports against those of its key trading partners and international competitors. East Asian economies export not only into the United States, but also into Europe and other Asia-Pacific economies. The strong nominal pegs to the U.S. dollar and low inflation rates indicate that competitiveness could not have been lost in the U.S. market. Could the East Asian economies have lost competitiveness against other competitors in markets other than the U.S.? Using measures of the "real effective exchange rate" would indicate if this was the case.

The available evidence suggests that "loss of competitiveness" is not an important explanation for the Asian economic crisis[23] and that the Asian currency crises, unlike those in transition economies, were not caused by the appreciation of the real exchange rates of national currencies. Chinn (1998) provides some econometric evidence consistent with this contention, albeit indirectly. The study utilizes a model-based determination of the equilibrium exchange rate, which takes into account the consistency of monetary policy and the nominal exchange rate. The analysis indicates that except for the Singapore dollar (which was estimated to have been overvalued by 45 per cent against the estimated equilibrium rate), none of the other East Asian currencies were grossly overvalued. The model relies heavily on a monetary sector determination of the equilibrium exchange rate and does not address the question of real sector competitiveness directly.

In arguing in favour of the loss of competitiveness explanation mention is made of the export slump that afflicted the East Asian economies in 1996 mostly induced by the overcapacity in the electronics sector. Previously, we had argued how falling export growth rates were an important consequence of the overvalued exchange rates in Russia and other crisis-afflicted transition economies. For these transition economies, the pattern is evident over a period of at least three years. In contrast, in East Asia, the export slump was only evident in 1996 and in this year there was a drastic fall, suggesting that external factors especially the cyclical slump in demand for electronics products, not internal factors were the cause. Singapore's exports grew by 25 and 22 per cent in 1994 and 1995, fell to 7 per cent in 1996. Malaysian exports grew by 23 and 26 per cent in 1994 and 1995, and grew only by 4 per cent in 1996. Thailand felt some competition for its labor-intensive exports and together with the electronics slump this translated into a zero export growth rate in 1996. In 1994 and 1995, Thai merchandise exports grew at rates of 22 and 25 per cent (Montes 1998*a*).

Overemphasizing the impact of the Asian export slump of 1996 suffers from a few weaknesses. First, it is generally agreed that the 1996 slump was strongly based on the electronics sector. In this sector, Southeast Asian economies are already a step ahead of the other new competitors in world markets. Emphasizing the loss of competitiveness as the cause of the crisis while recognizing the key role of the more advanced electronics sector undermines the competitiveness argument. The new competitors could not really have taken advantage of the supposedly overvalued exchange rate of the old competitors since the new competitors did not participate strongly in these advanced industries. The 1996 slump was based on an external demand slump.

Second, by 1997, a sharp recovery in electronics exports was evident. Thailand, because its exports were not as technologically weighted as those of Malaysia and Singapore, would have been more vulnerable. But its exports were recovering in 1997 and a competitiveness explanation cannot really explain why the prices of Thai equities began trending down earlier, in 1995, and continued trending down in 1997.

Third, this approach cannot really explain how Singapore and Malaysia were immediately drawn into the currency attacks in 1997. Before the crisis, there was a general belief that the Malaysian ringgit was undervalued and Malaysia could afford to let its currency appreciate faster.

Mention has also made of China's devaluation of the renminbi in 1994, which indicated a 50 per cent devaluation based on the official rates. However, China's exchange adjustment of 1994 can be more properly interpreted as a unification of the exchange rate, in which 60–80 per cent of its exports had already been transacted at "market rates". Under this view, China's actual devaluation in 1994 would have been in the order of 7–10 per cent, much smaller than the 30–50 per cent devaluations in Southeast Asian currencies.[24] Before 1994, the renminbi was implicitly depreciating as a consequence of the trend that an increasing proportion of Chinese external trade was being carried out at the alternative non-subsidized rate. These effective depreciations appeared to have been reasonably absorbed by the Southeast Asian economies, whose export growth rates until 1996 had been in double digits.

Mention is also made of the real exchange rate appreciation in the Asian economies in the 1990s during the era of capital inflows. Mention is continually made of the strong peg to the dollar of the Asian economies,[25] even after the dollar appreciated globally after mid-1996. Different estimates of the extent of real appreciation attest to a relatively modest rate of appreciation. Table 5.1, from Corsetti, Pesenti and Roubini (1998), suggest a maximum of 17 per cent real appreciation; for Thailand, the estimate is only 8 per cent; none of these are comparable to depreciations that have occurred in the crisis. For Mexico by 1994, the extent of real appreciation had been estimated by as much as 30 per cent (Edwards 1998). Figure 5 in Diel and Schweickert (1997), in paper which otherwise devotes a lot of discussion to the perils of pegged exchange rates, indicates the same modest real exchange appreciation for Thailand, Indonesia and Malaysia. Bond's (1998) real exchange rate estimates in a paper presented before the crisis conform to the same pattern.

In all of these estimates, the Philippine peso appreciates the most (except possibly for Singapore depending on the weights used in calculating real exchange rates), while Korea manages a real depreciation in the same period. As a proportion of GDP, the Philippines and Korea receive the least capital inflows in the period. Korea is a victim of the crisis despite its success in resisting exchange appreciation. Korea's success in resisting exchange appreciation owes much to the effectiveness of its controls against capital inflows until 1996 when it joined the Organization for Economic Co-operation and Development (OCED) and relaxed the restrictions on short-term external borrowings of its banks. The Philippines is an unwitting victim of the

TABLE 5.1
**Real Exchange Rate, 1990–96**
(Base 1990 average, end-of-year, higher values mean appreciation)

| | *1990* | *1991* | *1992* | *1993* | *1994* | *1995* | *1996* |
|---|---|---|---|---|---|---|---|
| Korea | 97.10 | 91.50 | 87.80 | 85.20 | 84.70 | 87.80 | 86.80 |
| Indonesia | 97.40 | 99.60 | 100.80 | 103.80 | 101.00 | 100.50 | 105.10 |
| Malaysia | 97.00 | 96.90 | 109.70 | 111.00 | 107.10 | 107.00 | 111.80 |
| Philippines | 92.30 | 103.10 | 107.10 | 97.40 | 111.60 | 109.50 | 116.00 |
| Singapore | 101.20 | 105.70 | 106.00 | 108.60 | 111.90 | 112.70 | 117.90 |
| Thailand | 102.20 | 99.00 | 99.70 | 101.90 | 98.30 | 101.70 | 107.60 |
| Hong Kong | 99.70 | 103.90 | 108.50 | 115.90 | 114.50 | 116.10 | 125.50 |

SOURCE: Table 11 of Corsetti, Pesenti, and Roubini (1998).

crisis (Montes 1998*c*), despite an apparent eagerness to participate as indicated by its exchange appreciation before the crisis. However, as another indication of the relative unimportance of the competitiveness explanation, the Philippine economy has not been as severely hurt by the external crisis.

After the crisis erupted, the resulting forced devaluations and collapses in domestic demand, coupled with difficulties in obtaining trade credits for imports, have sharply boosted current account surpluses among the East Asian economies. While the devaluations have improved the competitiveness of Southeast Asian economies, it cannot be argued in the converse that these adjustments were necessary to regain competitiveness.

In terms of macroeconomic management, the economies involved were accumulating reserves and being forced to continually adjust the composition of base money as they sought to maintain reasonable rates of monetary growth in the face of cumulating capital inflows (Montes 1998*a*).

To conclude, the story of the East Asian crises differs greatly from the crisis stories in transition economies, since most of the Asian currencies were not overpriced. While "first generation" currency crisis models developed by Krugman and described in Chapter 2, can provide the appropriate framework for explaining the mechanism of the currency crises in transition economies, these models offer little, if any, insights for the understanding of the Asian currency crises.

### Macroeconomic Fundamentals Explanation

A second possible explanation for the Asian currency crises is the presence of unsustainable borrowing and debt "fundamentals" based on the "second generation" model which we presented in Chapter 2. Currency attacks occur because there are parties who stand to make a capital gain when the international value of the currency changes. "First-generation models" justified these attacks based on the inconsistency of between a currency peg and flow deficits. In "second-generation" models (such as that in Obstfeld (1994), currency arrangements can be attacked even when "flow fundamentals", such as the level of government deficit or current account deficit, do not justify a change in the exchange rate, as long as parties can assume that the government gains from devaluation (in the form of the depreciation of the domestic debt denominated in national currency) net of losses (in the form of inflationary consequences and increased costs to service foreign debt). The crisis in Europe's 1992 ERM (Exchange Rate Mechanism) inspired these models.

Was the accumulation of the government indebtedness responsible for the currency crises in East Asia? Thailand had current account deficit of 8 per cent of GDP in 1996, the year of the export slump (Table 5.2) and this is the most often-cited case of unsustainable fundamentals in the region. Malaysia's current account deficit at about the same level has also been mentioned. The pattern of current account deficits has to be interpreted in the light of accumulated debt. For the East Asian economies, the level of external debt as a proportion to GDP were in the 50 per cent range for Indonesia and the Philippines (part of which had been accumulated from the 1980s debt crisis) and in the 30 to 40 per cent range for Malaysia and Thailand. These levels are lower than those seen in the Latin American economies in the 1980s debt crisis and certainly lower than for many of the countries joining the Euro-11 monetary union.

External financing stops for a country when it stops, but based on historical ranges of values, it should not have stopped for Malaysia in 1997. Malaysia's current account deficit was trending down and net short-term capital inflows were negative in 1996.

Based on historical ranges of values, an argument could have also been made that external financing did not have to stop for Thailand when it did in 1997. Based on long-term considerations of productivity growth, accumulated debt levels, levels of direct foreign investment, trends in the terms of trade, and robustness of government financing, Reisen (1997, p.12), in May 1997, made the judgement that Malaysian and Thai current account deficits "appear to be sustainable". The robustness of East Asian savings rates and fiscal finances, in absolute and relative (to those of other economies) terms, is argued in Montes (1998*a*). Montes and Abdusalamov (1998), based on data shown in Table 5.2, argue that for Indonesia, that the "fundamentals" were basically "sound".

In the case of Korea, until it lent out reserves to foreign subsidiaries in December, the economy could not have been vulnerable to a currency attacks. Thailand was quite vulnerable to a currency attack not directly because of its fundamentals but as a result of declining reserves as a consequence of the defence of the value of the baht to the dollar.

The Thai experience of a sudden loss of reserves compelling a devaluation has often been compared with that of Mexico before the 1994 crisis when Mexico had a fiscal surplus and a current account deficit of about the same size. There are, however, three key contrasts between the Thai and Mexican circumstances before their respective crises. First, the Mexican peso was more strongly overvalued (by as much as 30 per cent) while the baht was only modestly overvalued. Second, unlike the Mexican authorities which had been using the peg of the peso to reduce domestic inflation in the same way as the Russian authorities, the Thai authorities had not been using the baht peg to the dollar to reduce domestic inflation. Thailand did not have before the crisis, and even after it had devalued by fifty per cent, a domestic inflation problem, due to a longstanding tradition of conservative monetary policy coupled with highly flexible prices among domestic sectors. Third, the Thai economy, unlike the Mexican economy that was growing at less than 2 per cent per year in the years leading up to its crisis, was growing robustly before the crisis at around 8 per year.

## Weak Financial Sectors and Vulnerability to the Crisis

Just had been the case in the Southern Cone countries before 1981 and the Scandinavian countries before 1988, Southeast Asian financial systems had been weakened by the capital inflow in the 1990s and we suggest this to be fundamental cause of the crisis (Montes 1998*a*). We therefore interpret the origin of the Asian currency crisis as a mix of the private debt sector crisis and a domestic credit crisis under the condition of an open capital account.

TABLE 5.2
**Data on Macroeconomic Fundamentals, East Asian Countries, 1994–98**

| | *Thailand* | | | | | *Indonesia* | | | | | *Malaysia* | | | | |
|---|---|---|---|---|---|---|---|---|---|---|---|---|---|---|---|
| | *1994* | *1995* | *1996* | *1997* | *1998* | *1994* | *1995* | *1996* | *1997* | *1998* | *1994* | *1995* | *1996* | *1997* | *1998* |
| In Percent | | | | | | | | | | | | | | | |
| Real GDP Growth | 8.9 | 8.7 | 5.5 | –0.4 | –3.1 | 7.5 | 8.2 | 8.0 | 5.0 | –17.0 | 9.2 | 9.5 | 8.6 | 7.8 | 2.5 |
| CPI Inflation Rate | 5.1 | 5.8 | 5.9 | 5.6 | 10.1 | 8.5 | 9.4 | 7.9 | 6.6 | 39.1 | 3.7 | 3.4 | 3.5 | 2.7 | 5.1 |
| Money Supply Growth | 12.9 | 17.0 | 12.6 | 16.5 | 15.4 | 20.0 | 27.2 | 27.2 | 23.2 | | 14.7 | 24.0 | 20.9 | 22.6 | 16.1 |
| Saving/GDP | 34.9 | 34.3 | 33.1 | 31.8 | | 29.2 | 29.0 | 28.8 | 27.3 | | 32.7 | 33.5 | 36.7 | 37.0 | |
| Fiscal Balance/GDP | 2.0 | 2.6 | 1.6 | –0.4 | | 0.0 | 0.8 | 1.4 | 2.0 | | 2.5 | 3.8 | 4.2 | 1.6 | |
| Current Acct. Balance/GDP | –5.6 | –7.9 | –7.9 | –2.2 | 3.9 | –1.7 | –3.3 | –3.3 | –2.6 | 1.9 | –7.8 | –10.0 | –4.9 | –4.8 | –0.5 |
| Growth of Exports in US$ | 19.8 | 26.2 | –0.8 | 4.4 | 3.3 | 8.8 | 13.4 | 9.7 | 7.3 | –2.1 | 24.7 | 25.8 | 6.0 | 0.8 | –12.9 |
| External Debt/GDP | 45.8 | 49.7 | 49.3 | n.a. | | 61.0 | 61.5 | 56.7 | | | 40.4 | 39.3 | 40.1 | | |
| Short-term/External Debt | 44.5 | 49.4 | 41.4 | | | 18.0 | 20.9 | 25.0 | | | 21.1 | 21.2 | 27.8 | | |
| Official Reserves (US$ billion) | 29.3 | 36.0 | 37.7 | 26.2 | 28.6 | 12.1 | 13.7 | 18.3 | 16.6 | 15.5 | 25.4 | 23.8 | 27.0 | 21.7 | 20.4 |
| in months of imports | 6.5 | 6.1 | 6.2 | 5.0 | 7.9 | 4.5 | 4.0 | 5.1 | 4.8 | 7.7 | 5.1 | 3.7 | 4.1 | 3.3 | 3.7 |

| | Korea | | | | | Singapore | | | | | China | | | | |
|---|---|---|---|---|---|---|---|---|---|---|---|---|---|---|---|
| | 1994 | 1995 | 1996 | 1997 | 1998 | 1994 | 1995 | 1996 | 1997 | 1998 | 1994 | 1995 | 1996 | 1997 | 1998 |
| In Percent | | | | | | | | | | | | | | | |
| Real GDP Growth | 8.6 | 8.9 | 7.1 | 5.5 | –4.0 | 10.5 | 8.8 | 6.9 | 7.8 | 1.0 | 12.6 | 10.5 | 9.7 | 8.8 | 7.0 |
| CPI Inflation Rate | 6.3 | 4.5 | 4.9 | 4.5 | 8.8 | 3.1 | 1.7 | 1.4 | 2.0 | 1.0 | 21.7 | 14.8 | 6.1 | 1.5 | –2.1 |
| Money Supply Growth | 18.7 | 15.6 | 15.8 | 21.5 | 13.3 | 14.4 | 8.5 | 9.8 | 10.3 | 11.1 | 35.1 | 29.5 | 25.3 | 17.3 | 14.6 |
| Saving/GDP | 34.6 | 35.1 | 33.3 | 32.9 | | 49.8 | 50.0 | 50.1 | 50.0 | | 42.6 | 41.0 | 42.9 | 40.8 | |
| Fiscal Balance/GDP | 1.0 | 0.0 | 0.0 | 0.0 | | 13.7 | 12.0 | 8.4 | 8.3 | | –1.6 | –1.7 | –1.5 | 1.5 | |
| Current Acct. Balance/GDP | –1.2 | –2.0 | –4.9 | –2.0 | 5.5 | 17.1 | 16.8 | 15.7 | 15.2 | 14.3 | 1.4 | 0.2 | 0.9 | 2.4 | 2.1 |
| Growth of Exports in US$ | 16.8 | 30.3 | 3.7 | 5.0 | 7.0 | 30.5 | 22.5 | 5.8 | 0.0 | 9.9 | 31.9 | 22.9 | 1.5 | 20.9 | 23.9 |
| External Debt/GDP | 14.9 | 17.2 | 21.6 | | | 11.1 | | | | | 18.6 | 16.9 | 15.8 | | |
| Short-term/External Debt | | 58.3 | 42.4 | | | | | | | | 17.4 | 18.9 | 15.8 | | |
| Official Reserves (US$ billion) | 25.6 | 32.7 | 34.0 | 21.1 | 35.5 | 58.2 | 68.7 | 76.8 | 71.4 | 73.7 | 52.9 | 75.4 | 107.0 | 142.8 | 140.6 |
| in months of imports | 3.0 | 2.9 | 2.7 | 1.7 | 3.0 | 6.8 | 6.6 | 7.0 | 6.5 | 8.2 | 5.5 | 6.8 | 9.3 | 12.0 | 15.6 |

SOURCE: SAFCM [1998, Table 4, Appendix 4].

The approach we suggest is that which directly implicates the external *private* borrowing boom which follows a financial liberalization effort; the crisis is explained by the increasing fragility of the banking system that leaves the country vulnerable to a currency attack (Montes 1998*a*, Montes 1998*b*).

Dooley (1998) works out a model based on insurance considerations, starting from the presumption that governments of emerging economies stand behind the viability of their domestic banking system. Resident banks, households, and firms sell to non-residents "insured liabilities" for which the backing is the international reserves controlled by monetary authorities. When the size of these liabilities begins to exceed the net international reserves, then a currency attack must ensue as existing insurance claim owners try to cash in before the insurance fund runs out.

What provides the model its analytical fitness is the set of three conditions that Dooley suggests are necessary to be able to generate this process. First, governments must have net international reserves with which to back up the insurance offer. Dooley attempts to interpret the rise of "emerging" markets to be possible only with the appearance of net reserves that would provide the implicit insurance. Some key factors for the appearance of such reserves are the reduction in international interest rates and the debt write-offs from the Brady Bonds from the late 1980s that reduced the net international liabilities of certain countries.

The second condition is a credible commitment by the government to perform the insurance contract by exhausting these reserves. This means that the government will not default or devalue the currency before reserves are exhausted. The third factor is that private investors must be able to complete transactions that can produce insured losses.

The model can explain both a lending boom (as being sparked by the appearance of insurance assets) and a subsequent currency attack. It can explain the onset of a currency attack even when "fundamentals" do not change. The extent of the sudden reversal of capital flows to the Asian region is shown in Table 5.3.

One credible view of the Thai experience emphasizes the possibility that there might have been a large change in the implicit insurance provided by the authorities that made the currency attack that began in May 1997 succeed. This explanation says that there was change in the stance of many Asian governments with regard to contingent liabilities in ensuring the viability of the domestic financial system.[26]

In the first half of 1997, after successfully fending off currency attacks in November 1996 and February 1997, the Thai authorities began to more publicly and directly address the required adjustments in the domestic financial system. The weaknesses in the financial system had been a key motivation for delaying the currency depreciation in 1996, which would have caused widespread bankruptcies. In March 1997, Thai authorities publicly asked finance companies — which had been on the leading edge of systemic instability — to increase their capitalization, with a firm pledge that those that did not meet the requirements would have to close. This could be interpreted as a weakening of the implicit Thai guarantee behind the foreign exchange liabilities of domestic financial companies and might have provoked a more determined currency attack as happened beginning in May 1997.

Indonesian authorities tightened liquidity (in the context of an already weak banking system) as their response to the currency attacks after the Thai devaluation and before their first IMF programme. Then, there were the abrupt closures of finance companies (without a workout programme and

TABLE 5.3
**Shifts in Private Capital Flows by Country, 1994–98**
(in US$ billions)

| | *1994* | *1995* | *1996* | *1997* | *1998** | *1997 of % of GDP* |
|---|---|---|---|---|---|---|
| China | –8.3 | –13.5 | –17.8 | –25.3 | –38.0 | –3.4 |
| Hong Kong | 15.3 | 25.2 | 11.0 | 32.2 | 12.9 | 20.9 |
| Taiwan | 3.5 | –6.5 | –12.0 | –9.5 | –0.2 | –13.3 |
| Korea | 11.6 | 17.5 | 27.2 | –13.0 | –28.5 | –2.8 |
| Singapore | –6.1 | –8.5 | –7.2 | –15.5 | –28.5 | –2.8 |
| Malaysia | –1.7 | 1.3 | 2.8 | –14.0 | –6.4 | –14.2 |
| Thailand | 12.0 | 19.3 | 15.1 | –10.8 | –8.9 | –5.9 |
| Philippines | 2.7 | –0.1 | 7.8 | 0.3 | 1.0 | 0.4 |
| Indonesia | 2.1 | 4.8 | 4.9 | –6.7 | –8.7 | –3.0 |
| Japan | –84.0 | –31.9 | –10.9 | –53.4 | –57.0 | –1.2 |
| Asia ex. China | 39.4 | 52.9 | 48.8 | –36.9 | –34.2 | –2.7 |
| ASIA TOTAL | 31.2 | 39.4 | 31.0 | –62.2 | –87.9 | –2.9 |
| China & HK | 7.0 | 11.7 | –6.8 | 7.0 | –25.1 | 0.8 |

*Annual estimates extrapolated from January to April actuals.
SOURCE: Howell [1998, Figure 13].

protection for depositors) under the IMF programmes in Thailand (in August 1997) of 16 commercial banks in Indonesia (October 1997) and of the merchant banks in Korea (in January 1998). All of these actions preceeded a drastic drop in the demand for domestic currency denominated assets.

In the case of Korea, it appears that the state's implicit insurance had actually been increased in the month of the crisis, when the authorities assigned part of the country's international reserves to foreign branches of Korean banks. When the investment withdrawals continued even with this guarantee, the currency crisis erupted.

The vulnerability of Asian economies to currency attack can be attributed to the size of their short-term liabilities relative to international reserves. Table 5.4 indicates that the three Asian crisis countries had the highest ratios of short-term debt (to Bank for International Settlements [BIS] banks) to international reserves. This lesson had already been strongly implicated in the Mexican crisis of 1994 (Calvo and Mendoza 1996) and was a lesson unapplied both by governments and private investors to Southeast Asia.

It is difficult to differentiate between two explanations for the continued accommodation of short-term borrowing to Thailand. Dooley's (1998) model would say that Thailand still had enough net reserves to service the increases in short-term debt. Another explanation would be myopia and herd behavior on the part of external investors (Montes 1998*a*). The information required to strike the ratio between short-term liabilities (from the BIS) and international reserves (from the national central banks) had been publicly available and should encouraged an earlier and gentler withdrawal of short-term financing. In contradiction, sovereign premia for the afflicted countries continued to fall in the months before the Thai devaluation.

If the weakened financial system provided the vulnerability to the crisis, the successful currency attack could have only magnified this vulnerability. McKinnon and Pill (1998, p. 27) argue that:

> Rather than helping to cure the problem through monetary easing as in Mexico, devaluation exacerbated the underlying cause of the crisis, namely the fragility and vulnerability of the domestic financial sector. In retrospect, the countries of Southeast Asia may have been better served by more aggressive defense of their currency pegs — presumably aided by earlier and greater support from the international financial community.

TABLE 5.4
**Liabilities to BIS Banks as of June 1997**

| | *Total Liability (US$ bill.)* | *Short-term Liability (US$ bill.)* | *Short-term/ Total (pct)* | *Total Liability/ G D P (pct)* | *Short-Term/ Reserves (pct)* |
|---|---|---|---|---|---|
| ASEAN | | | | | |
| Indonesia | 58.7 | 34.7 | 59.1 | 26.5 | 162.9 |
| Malaysia | 28.8 | 16.3 | 56.6 | 29.3 | 60.9 |
| Philippines | 14.1 | 8.3 | 58.9 | 16.2 | 72.6 |
| Thailand | 69.4 | 45.6 | 65.7 | 38.1 | 141.1 |
| | | | | | |
| Other Asia | | | | | |
| China | 57.9 | 30.1 | 52.0 | 7.1 | 23.4 |
| Korea | 103.4 | 70.2 | 67.9 | 21.3 | 210.6 |
| Taiwan | 25.2 | 22.0 | 87.3 | 9.2 | 24.3 |
| | | | | | |
| Latin America | | | | | |
| Argentina | 44.4 | 23.9 | 53.8 | 15.8 | 130.3 |
| Brazil | 71.1 | 44.2 | 62.2 | 9.6 | 77.2 |
| Chile | 17.6 | 7.6 | 43.2 | | |
| Colombia | 17.0 | 6.7 | 39.4 | | |
| Mexico | 62.1 | 28.2 | 45.4 | 18.5 | 118.7 |
| Venezuela | 12.1 | 3.6 | 29.8 | | |

SOURCE: Ito [1998, Table 1].

Thailand, of course, ran out of reserves (and less than a dozen people in the world knew about it until the devaluation [Bardacke 1998]) and so did Korea in late November 1997. Indonesia devalued early (i.e., kept its reserves) in July 1997 but the continued fall in the rupiah incapacitated its weakened financial (and corporate) sector, nevertheless. It also approached the IMF early.

## Corruption, Transparency, and Accountability as Explanations

Socio-politico-legal explanations have dominated the journalistic explanations of the Asian crisis, perhaps because these are most readily understandable to the general public. The calls against "korupsi, kolusi and nepotismi" (KKN) in the midst of political changes and the political movements in East Asia which the crisis has spawned find resonance in this explanation. Unfortunately, these explanations also seem to be the redoubt into which the Washington consensus has sought refuge, so that defects in accountability, transparency, and governance in the capital importing (as opposed to in the capital exporting) economies eventually get "punished" by somehow anthromorphic, singularly conscious, markets.

In contrast with the socio-politico-legal accounts of the Latin American debt crisis of the 1980s which relied on the assumed intrinsic investment inefficiencies of public enterprises, Asian governments' coddling of private business groups is implicated in the Asian crisis. This accusation converts the virtue of East Asian government-business co-ordination of the World Bank (1993) into a vice.

Siamwalla (1998) discusses how in 1994 Thai regulatory authorities failed to end the at times criminal lending practices of the small Bangkok Bank of Commerce by obtaining a seat on the board; the regulatory representative simply got voted out of the board. When a run on the bank developed, $7 billion in funds had to be injected. In Indonesia, the lack of procedures in dealing with potential bank failures effectively meant that all banks operated under a full guarantee from Bank Indonesia (Montes and Abdusalamov 1998). In a situation in which almost all prominent bankers and business groupings were allies if not relatives of the President of Indonesia, it is not surprising that the two largest bank failures before 1997 were owned by businessmen closely associated with the government.

In Korea, the practice of cross guaranteeing loans within *chaebols* along with the non-existence of consolidated financial statements represented that economy's notion that the reputation of a borrower dominates all other loan criteria. This was workable (and relatively benign) in the earlier days of the development process and when access to foreign funds was limited on the supply side.

In Japan, the practice of changing uncooperative accountants and collusive practices in providing credit apparently survived even as Japan became a dominant industrial nation. As the crisis unfolded, the deficiencies of untested or non-existent bankruptcy procedures came to be associated with the poor credit practices in Asia.

The socio-politico-legal explanation is certainly important and one that hypothetically promises permanent improvements in accounting standards and hopefully accountability, in transparency and hopefully freedom of speech and inquiry, and wider participation in decision-making and hopefully democratization. Even if one does not accept the Anglo-Saxon ideals in which these standards are imagined, Asian societies, with growing middle classes and increasing international interaction, had been moving in these directions. The crisis has released domestic pressures that can accelerate these trends, as long as a backlash can be avoided and the crisis does not soak up all the resources that would be needed to continue these trends.

But does this hypothesis really offer a sharp enough analytical knife for understanding the Asian crisis? If there was anything specific to Asia in regard to poor credit practices, it would be that the original crisis countries all had savings rates near or over 30 per cent of GDP and, except for the Philippines, minimal indications of capital flight. From a logical point of view, and if one believed in the postulated declining marginal efficiency of investment, stories about corruption and disreputable credit practices would be of great interest journalistically but would be unnecessary to predict the eventual collapse of an overextended credit system based on bad lending. As the supply of good local investment projects diminished, Asia's surfeit of savings were increasingly being invested poorly, even as foreign investors sought to participate in the investment frenzy. Growth in the East Asian economies could have remained the highest among developing countries without the additional foreign resources financial liberalization might have brought (Kwan 1997) and the problem might, instead, have been that not enough of Asia's own savings took flight before the crisis.

The same pattern of boom-to-bust to crisis had occurred earlier in the Southern Cone countries (Chile, Argentina, Uruguay) of Latin America in 1981–82 and in three Scandinavian countries (Norway, Sweden, Finland) in 1990–92 (Montes 1998*a*). In the aftermath of these earlier crises, an endless stream of similar stories of shady practices, poor regulatory capability, unfortunate bailouts of early cases, inadequate accounting and reporting practices, exploitation of the deregulation process by large business groupings such as *grupos economicos* in Chile and *conglomerasi* in Indonesia surfaced. For these cases and for the Asian case, one can make the argument that these weaknesses had been there before the problems that actually precipitated the actual crisis — the boom in credit expansion fed by external finance. Under this hypothesis, the blame on Asian policy-makers and their Bretton Woods partners would have to lie in not learning lessons from these earlier episodes.

However, the recycling of earlier recriminations, theoretically safe as it is and apparently costless on the part of creditor countries, also has an insidious impact on policy design and the conduct of international relations. It places great emphasis on what economists like to call "structural reforms", which are important in any successful development process. However, they are more difficult to complete in a time of macroeconomic, not to mention social, distress when the demands on bureaucratic capacity have risen considerably, if only from the number of foreign expert teams visiting the capital (Feldstein 1998). It discourages the early infusion of liquidity and the temporary imposition of debt standstills or capital controls (on the grounds that these policies will deflate the pressure for reform); liquidity infusions have depended on performance on reform promises.

Consider that at the present juncture Indonesia[27] is carrying out a 6-month crash programme to install bankruptcy procedures as part of its structural reform programme. In most other societies, bankruptcy procedures have evolved through practice and precedent because these require not only the balancing of interest between debtors and creditors but also the infusion of the social interest in protecting production, employment and physical capital. In Indonesia, the structural reform programme has required the rapid installation of new bankruptcy laws and regulations (involving a certain amount of haphazard copying of foreign procedures which has apparently resulted in a procedure that unduly favours creditors). The completion of training of 12 judges and the start-up of training of the requisite number of lawyers and accountants is part of this programme.

Because the exchange rate has made ninety per cent of enterprises listed in the stock exchange and almost all banks technically bankrupt, the scale of the Indonesian bankruptcy practice promises to be extensive. In each case, individual creditors and debtors must decide if they want to participate in the hothouse creation of Indonesian bankruptcy traditions based on their self-interest, the currency composition of their personal and corporate portfolios, and on their projections of what the rupiah-dollar exchange rate will be. If Indonesia succeeds in meeting its reform promises in activating these bankruptcy practices in the midst of wide-ranging political and social pressures, it stands the risk of having an overly developed bankruptcy capacity after the crisis. If, instead, liquidity had been injected early enough or if other direct measures to stabilize the rupiah had been put in place,[28] the scale of bankruptcies would not be as high and Indonesia would not be facing the risk of post-crisis overcapacity in bankruptcy procedures. But such an approach would not be proper under this socio-politico-legal explanation of the crisis.

There are legitimate reasons to worry about casualness in the matter of changing of governments, in widespread bankruptcies, or in the implementation of austerity programmes. Economic non-linearities (that large political and economic events drastically change economic structures and incentives and government capacity) and asymmetries (it is easier to see a company go bankrupt than to wait upon the start-up of a firm that would replace it) can make economic recovery unnecessarily distant (Stiglitz 1998).

It is also important to point out the subtle but important difference in the "corruption" explanation as it is applied in the East Asian economies, where tax collection rates continued to be robust and fiscal deficits low, savings rates high, and indications of capital flight before the crisis minimal.

While, for example, before the crisis the series of Russian current account surpluses in the context of low savings rates, low tax collection rates, and large government deficits might indicate short-horizons on the part of Russian investors feeding capital flight, such a "carpetbagging" emphasis is difficult to associate with East Asian investment. Investment projects in East Asia, occurring in economies with rising property values and high economic growth rates, certainly had perceptible element of collusion in pricing and loan approval. However, for the most part, the projects that obtained loans were genuinely expected to be operational and produce a cash flow.

Even in an investment climate dominated by short-term horizons, incentives to cannabilize and dismantle productive assets, and capital flight, the roles of an overvalued exchange rate and that of the ease in transferring wealth abroad afforded by liberalized capital markets cannot be overemphasized. In Russia, the overvalued exchange rate undermined the prospects of industrial enterprises whose output would have to compete against imported goods.

The other beguiling aspect of the socio-politico-legal explanation is that it draws an iron curtain over other policies that might have been appropriate in avoiding the Asian crisis and in preventing similar crises in the future. It tends to excuse the recklessness on the external creditor side while creating suspicions over various capital controls as devices that hide domestic poor lending practices.

## A Generalized Run on Asian Assets

The generalized retreat of capital from Asian economies inflicted currency devaluations not just in the countries with weak financial systems but also in countries with relatively healthy financial sectors such as those of Singapore and Hong Kong. The impact on other countries of the continued uncertainty in Asia was an increase in the cost of their international borrowing. This affected Latin America, Russia, and other East European countries.

The policy implication of such a view of the Asian crisis is that providing liquidity very early and in massive amounts might have reduced the depth and spread of the crisis. Under this view, the response to the Asian crisis should have followed along the lines of the 1994 version of the Mexican crisis. In that crisis, the size of the response was swift, large, and practically unconditional; the scale of funds ensured that Mexico's dollar denominated debt that was immediately due (the *tesobonos*) was wound down four months after the crisis began (Montes 1998*d*). The size of the package bent the IMF rules beyond their limits and forced the European directors of the IMF to abstain from voting for it. The reflow of funds into Mexico was so significant that Mexico was able to repay the standby loan ahead of schedule, and permitted Mexico to delay the decision on absorbing the resulting non-performing loans of the financial system until October 1998.

The contrast with the Asian experience (and the attempted Brazilian rescue in early November 1998) could not have been starker. The Asian programmes were heavily conditional. The festooning of conditionality in these programmes provided symbols against which investment managers could measure the riskiness of their exposure to each economy[29] and this frenzy became particularly noisy, and then incongruously tragic, for Indonesia. A proposal for a $100 billion exchange stabilization fund in September 1998 was immediately vetoed by the United States and the IMF. The uncontrolled currency collapses instigated a second round of increases in corporate bankruptcies and increases in non-performing loans in the financial system. Tight liquidity and the headlong closing of financial institutions in

Thailand, Indonesia, and Korea compounded real sector disintegration and fed into the currency collapses.

The course of the crisis revealed a new feebleness in single-country programmes suggesting that perhaps not all the distress in the Asian economies can be traced to domestic factors or to policy mistakes. The crisis, intensifying as it did in a matter of months, re-exposed the harmful non-existence of debt workout procedures, standstill possibilities and inability of the IMF to lend into arrears. These deficiencies had already been commented on during the 1980s debt crisis. The lack of a liquidity provider of last resort, or the inability of the Asian countries to overcome the political objections to create such a provider for the region, was another insight.

# 6
# THE FUTURE OF GLOBALIZED CAPITAL MARKETS

The accelerating global integration of financial markets is not, by itself, the cause of the currency collapses, and their attendant economic crises. As should be implicit in the discussion in this volume, it is more important to evaluate the manner in which countries integrate themselves into these markets. We have suggested dissimilar causes for the different types of integration among the countries that have been afflicted by the crisis.

The accelerating integration of these markets has the potential of increasing the frequency and the magnitude of these crises. If there is a single insight that can be derived from the East Asian facet of the crisis, it is that even the seemingly successful globalizers undertake significant risks when they internationalize their capital markets.

This section catalogues a set of policy implications in an environment where international capital and currency markets provide an opportunity at the same time that they create vulnerabilities for emerging economies. This global economic crisis in the last decade of the 20th century suggests two cautionary lessons. First, that the hypothetical abundance of private external capital can finance unsustainable policies, in particular overvalued exchange rates and the progressive weakening of domestic credit markets. Second, there was a clear danger that private international capital flows would overwhelm the capacity of public authorities to contain self-fulfilling panic.

The policy lessons for transition economies and other similar economies undertaking market reforms which have almost instantly given them access to foreign capital resources, are also twofold. First, they need to avoid real exchange rate appreciation that led to current currency crises. Second, given that they find themselves in a trend of increasing external indebtedness, they have to draw early lessons from more complex government debt crisis (Latin American countries in early 1980s) and private sector debt crisis (Southeast Asia in 1997–98) to avoid another episode of currency collapses in the near future.

### Preventing Excessive Overvaluation of the Domestic Currency

In a story with numerous precedents, we have argued that overvaluation of the currency was the principal cause behind the Russian crisis. As in Mexico before 1994, monetary policies had been conservative and the exchange rate was being utilized as an inflation "anchor". However, as was the case in the Southern Cone countries of Latin America before their crises in 1982, an underlying and deep-seated fiscal deficit instigated a rising trend of borrowing, even though it is clear that by the time the Russian macroeconomic programme disintegrated, the level of external debt was within acceptable limits. At the prevailing exchange rate, which undermined the surplus on current account and galvanized capital flight, the dependence of the Russian economy on the external financing for its day-to-day operations was getting out of hand.

What unravelled was the exchange rate regime in the face of continuing capital flight and an ineluctable trend towards current account deterioration. Currency overvaluation lay behind both of these trends. The Russian case illustrates once again the limitations and the policy temptations of using the exchange rate as an anti-inflation instrument. Using the exchange rate as an anti-inflation anchor desensitizes it from developments in the real sector. Maintaining a strong peg at an overvalued level subsidizes capital flight and imports, and handicaps domestic production and exports; these circumstances tend to exacerbate the extent of overvaluation as long as the authorities are successful in using the exchange rate as an anchor.

Bringing inflation down to single digits in transition and other emerging market economies with a lot of market imperfections and structural rigidities is by itself a questionable policy. True, in countries with highly inflationary environment, chances are high that output growth will be weak, if any. However, it is generally recognized that a 40 per cent a year inflation is sort of a threshold. There is no evidence that inflation, as long as it is below 40 per cent annually, is automatically ruinous for growth, and there is even some evidence that inflation below 20 per cent a year may be beneficial (see Bruno and Easterly 1995; Bruno 1995; Stiglitz 1998).

It may be even argued that the threshold for transition economies is actually higher than that for other emerging markets because of the numerous inherited structural rigidities. In most successful reformers, inflation was by no means insignificant: it never fell below 20 per cent a year in the first 5 years of transition in Hungary, Poland and Slovenia, while in China, though it was low most of the time, there were outbursts of inflation in 1988–89 and in 1993–95, when it increased to about 20 per cent.

It seems that in this respect the Russian authorities went from one extreme (very high inflation of 1992–94) to the other, trying to be "more Catholic than the Pope", as it were in regard to inflation. After the exchange rate-based stabilization programme was enacted in 1995, it was pursued with greater diligence than elsewhere: right before the crisis, in July 1998, the year-to-year inflation was brought to the lowest level of 6 per cent — less than in most transition economies. This low level of inflation did impose unnecessary strains on the economy, causing the avalanche of non-payments and leading to the lack-of-demand-induced reduction of output. In fact, after the modest growth in 1997, output started to decline in the first half of 1998.

If authorities were to accept higher inflation rates and the gradual depreciation of the nominal rate, extreme overvaluation can be avoided. We have argued that the temptation to use the exchange rate as an anti-inflation instrument for too long and to attempt to achieve an overly low level of inflation is often too irresistible. When the sentiment of foreign creditors and nationals shifts and the belief becomes prevalent that authorities will be unable to defend the exchange rate, it becomes all the more difficult for authorities to abandon the peg, lest a currency freefall results. When the international reserves "run out" as a result of defending the currency, the peg has to be abandoned and the dreaded currency freefall ensues.

## Containing Private Irrational Exuberance and Enforcing Prudential Regulation

Emerging markets built their reputations with foreign creditors based on their intended liberalization programmes, which, when put in place, would reduce the hand of the government in economic life. These programmes cannot be implemented, much less designed, overnight. For example, legislation and implementing rules have to be determined; the design of these programmes have to take into account interactions with existing laws and longstanding traditions.

Even when the programmes are implemented, their positive impact will take years to begin to be felt.

The abruptly heightened ability of emerging economies to obtain external financing arises from expectations that these programmes will be implemented and bear positive fruit. The willingness of external financiers with limited information to make a bet on the future of these economies is commendable (except for the fact that, as discussed below, these activities are heavily tinged with moral hazard). However, the just-as-sudden and abrupt withdrawal of investment, by international funds, once again based on limited information, when they make an opposite judgement over the complex process of economic reform, is lamentable.

In the Asian economies in the 1990s up to the very day when Thailand devalued, irrational exuberance fed investment and credit activity. The increase in lending activity itself fed this exuberance, and for a while it appeared that the optimism was rational since growth provides for rising equity and land values, on which the collateral for lending is based. Governments, who are naturally loathe to prick activity that it does not have to finance, have to be particularly mindful of the need to watch against asset bubbles and move against these in time.

Taiwan, a few years back, had a particularly severe asset bubble which the government had the temerity to deflate. Singapore imposed restrictions and fees on property resales early in 1996. Thailand's property and equity bubble began deflating before the crisis, but this development promised dire distress for the domestic financial system. Just like Japanese authorities (who have even taken longer to address the same type of bubble), Thai authorities were in a forebearance mood when the currency attack on the baht succeeded in July 1997.

Pricking asset bubbles can be done independently of prudential regulation, though it requires a brave and strong government. Now we turn to prudential regulation, a capacity which all economies with a financial sector should have.

The importance of prudential regulatory capacity and practice before an extensive liberalization is, by now, a piece of vulgar wisdom and is often dollied up in sophisticated language within discussions of "sequencing". These lessons had been extensively discussed in the wake of the Southern Cone financial calamities in the early 1980s (Diaz-Alejandro 1985), McKinnon (1988) and had still not been learned by advisers to Asian governments by the late 1990s. The main proposition here is that since the markets for financial instruments are markets in promises to return money in the future they are especially susceptible to explosive, non-equilibrium, growth.

The basic principle that we would like to suggest here is that countries should be permitted, depending on their specific circumstance, to delay removal of various restrictions (such as interest rate ceilings, which prods lenders to lend only to safer borrowers or capital inflow controls, which prevents borrowers from having access to seemingly unlimited low-cost foreign finance) when prudential supervisory capacity is feeble.

There are lessons to be learned about the adequacy of prudential regulations for the transition economies as well. In Russia, for instance, the credit and banking crisis, as was argued in Chapter 4, was by no means necessary and was in fact manufactured by the poor crisis response (the government default on its short term debt and the central bank measures that undermined the credibility of commercial banks). Nevertheless, no matter from where the blow came, the onset of the crisis exposed the long-known and discussed weaknesses of the Russian domestic banking system. In a sense, the experience indicates that next time, when the shock might come from international capital flows, Russian banks would not be able to withstand it unless prudential regulations are tightened and a viable banking sector is created. Meanwhile, the continuation of the Russian policy of uncontrolled openness to capital flows appears to be an invitation for trouble, as it was in the Asian cases.

## Forcing Private Actors to Internalize Sovereign Risk

More flexible exchange rates are needed not only to elicit needed real sector adjustments, they are also needed to force private borrowers and lenders to take into account the risk of exchange rate adjustments.

In East Asia, domestic financial companies did not internalize the currency risk they were undertaking in intermediating foreign currency resources into domestic currency denominated loans. The strength of domestic currencies encouraged unhedged private foreign lending. The economist's temptation is to accuse the Southeast Asian authorities of pegging the currency too strongly at an overvalued level and to suggest that they should have allowed currencies to fall earlier. However, in a situation of overfinancing and falling sovereign premia all the way to July 1997, one might have also accused the authorities of insufficient tolerance of currency appreciation. Both accusations are correct and speaks to the need for the need for a certain amount currency flexibility to force private sector players to internalize currency risk. Chilean authorities, within a managed float system, have been adding noise to the exchange rate (Montes 1998*b*).

True, flexible exchange rates are a costly to importers and exporters and this provides a limit to such a policy (Grobar 1993). However, given the relatively small size of most emerging market economies and their rapidly growing, but their incomplete integration into the world economy, floating exchange rates may provide more flexibility for adjusting to the external shocks. Most developing and transition economies, with the exception of the smallest ones, like Hong Kong, Singapore (and perhaps Baltic states) are large enough to remain only partly exposed to world market conditions and hence can retain some inflexibility of domestic prices with respect to the world market prices. However, these same economies are not large enough to create an appropriate cushion in the form of foreign exchange reserves, to reduce the vulnerability from the international capital flows to reasonable levels. In most emerging markets (with the possible exception of China), foreign exchange reserves are normally enough to withstand at most several weeks, if not days of the attack on the currency. Beyond that and in light of the fact that the major international banks, investment and hedge funds operate with pools of money comparable to or even exceeding the value of reserves in most countries, fluctuations of the exchange rate remain the only reliable and efficient safety valve providing protection from external shocks.

Rigidly fixed exchange rates effectively force emerging economies to abandon their independent monetary policy so that they are doomed to adjust to the inflows and outflows of capital through real sector adjustments. When the exchange rate is pegged and prices are not completely flexible, changes in the money supply (caused by the fluctuation of reserves) may affect output rather than prices. The recent experience of East Asian and transition economies suggests that this kind of real sector adjustment is quite costly. To put it in the simplest form, under fixed exchange rate regime, neither changes in foreign exchange reserves, nor domestic price changes in response to money supply fluctuations provide enough room for manœuvre for handling international capital flows.

## Improving Information Usage and Transparency

In the emerging economies, aggressive lending behaviour before the crisis was abetted (but not caused) by poor accounting practices, incentives to conceal gains from tax authorities and losses from prudential regulators, weak traditions in independence of accounting practitioners, and limited traditions in internal controls in private companies. Hiding losses from regulators by assigning bad loans to another related company (a practice called "parking" during the junk bond days in the U.S. and called *tobashi*, "flinging away" during the Japanese asset bubble) became widespread.

More information is supposed to stabilize market behaviour. However, more information is merely more information. Before the crisis, the information already available should have already provided warning signals; one might argue that as early as late 1995 when signs of overbuilding in Bangkok were evident the Thai sovereign premium should have increased. "In actual fact a great deal of information usually turns out to be available which no one ever looked at or analysed. For transparency to be useful, people need to actually want to look — and too often those who are making high profits would rather not hear bad news" (Rivlin 1998).

## Providing for Different Levels of Capital Account Openness

Completely liberalized capital accounts are not appropriate for all economies and there is a need to work out international regimes to help countries productively operate illiberal capital account regimes.

One alternative would be to have 3 or 4 grades of open capital accounts, from the most illiberal to the most liberal. Economies with the highest rating would be designated as those with the greatest capacity to absorb private capital, including those from the most prickly investors; economies with the lowest rating should not be permitted to accept more volatile capital inflows. The presumption is that economies with the highest rating can receive more capital inflows at lower spreads. Economies would be allowed to graduate to the next grade only if they have put in place sufficient capacity in prudential supervision and macroeconomic management.

Incentive incompatibilities make it difficult to rely exclusively on using guarantees and fees to implement this grading scheme: giving more generous guarantees on more liberal systems is an intervention with the wrong sign. Controls have to used and a list has to devised which would tell all fund managers which types of controls are appropriate for which grade of openness and therefore do not have to be construed as a defense of a disappearing level of international reserves.

At the level of principle, one might like to support illiberal controls when

(1) they are justified by the requirements of prudential regulation and
(2) they are supportive of macroeconomic stability.

The actual situation is that many countries, including Uganda and Kenya but not including China and Viet Nam, already have convertible capital accounts in the wake of their liberalization programmes. In the case of Korea, the IMF structural adjustment programme entailed the precipitous opening of the capital account, which Korea's accession to the OECD was supposed to have liberalized in a phased manner.[30]

Open capital accounts do severely constrain exchange rate targeting and monetary policy. But the problem is less in the impossibility but in exploiting independence where it exists and creating the independence through national policy and international cooperation where it does not (Montes 1996). For example, domestic bonds are not perfect substitutes for international bonds and, because of their interest arbitrage will not necessarily remove all independent policy with regard to exchange rate setting. It is also important to distinguish policies and controls during periods of net capital inflows and during periods of net capital flight. Capital controls against outflows have often proved ineffective. However, because of market imperfections and the small size of domestic financial markets, controls against inflows, especially those of a short-term nature, might prove to be more effective. Bond markets and equity markets in emerging markets are typically small and secondary markets are not well-developed. This is the reason why in the crisis situation, international portfolio movements have such an immediate and decisive impact on exchange rates.

Creating the space for national policy with regard to exchange rate setting and monetary policy during non-crisis situations and with the aim of preventing the onset of crisis situations will require the application of capital account taxes and controls. It is certainly the case that countries must choose to accept smaller capital inflows and lower growth with these restrictions. The choice of these capital account restrictions will depend on the specific country, its own objectives, and its administrative capacity to implement these restrictions.

For transition economies, where the currency crises, as we argued in Chapter 3 were not triggered by debt and lending booms, there is an important lesson to be derived from the East Asian experience. As debt levels, both government and private in these economies continue to grow, measures should be taken to ensure that the soundness and reliability of banking institutions is not overrun by the openness of the capital accounts.

## Discouraging Reliance on Short-term Capital Flows

Capital account taxes and regulations should lean against short-term inflows in the capital account. Montiel and Reinhart (1997) provide some cross-country evidence that various combinations of reserve requirements and controls can change the composition of capital inflows. One famous approach is the non-remunerated Chilean reserve requirement of one year for all new capital inflows, including new trade credits.[31] This requirement effectively taxed inflows through lost interest earnings and have taxed more those inflows that stayed more briefly.

The problem is that there are a myriad of policies and regulations that actually subsidize short-term capital flows. For example, the Basle capital adequacy requirements provides only 20 per cent weighting for short-term lending from industrial economies to developing countries and requires a 100 per cent weighting for long-term lending. Such an implicit subsidy to short-term lending might be justified in terms of protecting depositors in industrial economies but, as the Asian crisis indicates, it can create instability in the international financial markets.

Equally potentially damaging are national policies that encourage short-term borrowing from abroad. The Bangkok International Banking Facility (BIBF) was basically financed from short-term dollar deposits, ninety-five per cent of which was onlent in domestic currency (Montes 1998*a*). Korean capital account controls had long been motivated by the need to control direct foreign investment and minimize the extent to which foreigners could obtain control of Korean enterprises. When Korea acceded to the OECD, it began, not by opening up the capital account for direct foreign investment and for long-term investment, but by liberalizing the ability of Korean banks to borrow on a short-term basis from abroad. This provided the proximate cause to the large runup in short-term debt of Korean commercial banks in the year before the Thai crisis.

## Minimizing Moral Hazard in International Lending

Improving the stability of international capital flows would also depend on drastic revision of the incentive structures affecting actors lending internationally, be they from the industrial economies or from other developing countries. Over-borrowing on the part of the afflicted countries requires an equivalent amount of overlending on the part of capital-surplus countries.

It is almost a whimsical feature of current discussions revolving around proposed economic surveillance procedures that the fragility of lending institutions be also included among vulnerability indicators of borrowing economies. It has a real basis: the termination by Japanese banks of Korean credit lines in November 1997 following the failure of the Takushoku Bank in Hokkaido was an important trigger of the Korean crisis. The main point is that public policy in the lending side is also important.

Before the crisis, BIS guidelines on capital adequacy requirements provided an implicit subsidy for short-term international lending from OECD banks to emerging economies. More damaging, incentive structures for international lenders have been insidious because lenders have not been taken into account for their poor lending practices. During the debt crisis of the 1980s, it took deposit money banks in the industrial economies almost a decade to begin recognizing their losses through the Brady Bond procedure.

In the current crisis, with a richer menu of lending (bank short-term credit, bank longer-term credit, bonds, and equity) than in the 1980s debt crisis, the old-fashioned method of IMF rescue creates a particularly corrupting hierarchy. Bank short-term credits are rescued almost completely, while those investors that committed more long-term funds (bank long-term credit, bonds, and equity) suffered greater losses. Thus, the more unstable capital inflows are rewarded by the standing rescue approaches.

Griffith-Jones (1998) discusses the different possibilities of improving the regulation at the source side. More regulation of the relatively unregulated investment funds, requiring better and more public disclosure of risk for example, would be justified by the post-crisis applications of taxpayer resources through the IMF and through bilateral loans. There are also proposals for cash reserve requirements for mutual funds are their exposure to more risky economies increases.

Soros (1997) suggests the establishment of an international regime to counter the over-investment followed by over-withdrawal syndrome as seen in Asia. This would consist of an "International Credit Insurance Corporation" that would guarantee international loans for each country for a modest fee. The amount of loans the authority would guarantee for each country would be based on its judgement on the ability of countries to service the debt.

# Concluding Comments

The total costs of the economic crises in East Asia, in Russia, and in the other transition economies remain to be tallied. Economic contraction of about 6 per cent is likely for 1998 for economies such as Thailand, Korea, Russia, and perhaps for Malaysia; for Indonesia the forecast for output contraction in 1998 is in the order of 15 per cent. Other economies which have also suffered currency devaluations and investment withdrawals have also been affected through sharply lower growth rates; among these we must count Singapore and the Philippines. These output declines will be experienced as will job losses and diminished medium-term income prospects for the populations of the affected countries. Business confidence and investment activities will only recover with the restoration of these prospects.

In specific countries, such as Indonesia and Russia, there will also be a period of political uncertainty. For these countries, a sharp recovery is not expected for 1999. Growth declines will moderate for most East Asian economies in 1999, but will still be significantly lower than previously experienced rates of growth. It is likely that Russian economic output will fall in the order of 5 per cent in 1999.

To these costs we must add, the costs of rehabilitating the financial system and the corporate sector. Estimates in the order of 20 per cent of GDP for Thailand and Korea are common, while estimates of about 30 per cent to as high as

50 per cent have been made for Indonesia. In Russia the cost of restructuring the banking sector heavily affected by the crisis is estimated as 45 billion roubles, about 15 per cent of total money supply. These costs will be spread out in the medium-term and as long as the reflow of private capital does not occur these costs will represent a drag on investment (in terms of higher cost) and economic recovery.

We have seen the era of abundant finance for transition economies. Yet these emerging markets have turned into a environment of capital flight and instability, capsizing those economies that had previously been so assiduously courted by foreign investors. Private investors have suddenly become overly pessimistic and nervous after the reckless credit expansion in the early 1990s. This unwarranted sudden reversal and the costs of the current crisis should generate the political will to intensify the search for more stable international financial institutions and more effective domestic macroeconomic policies.

# Notes

1. In a purely domestic economy, or a "closed" economy, *high inflation*, in which a domestic currency rapidly loses value relative to other domestic assets and consumption goods, would be a form of a currency crisis. In such a situation, other measures of value, such as the value of precious metals, emerge and in many cases, these replace the currency as the means of payment.
2. The fiscal deficits arise because typically the sterilization policy is carried out by selling bonds domestically at interest rates sufficiently high to attract buyers while depositing the proceeds of the sale in the purchase foreign bonds which pay lower interest rates.
3. Obstfeld (1994) presents the standard model.
4. These figures are derived from Table 10(2) of SAFCM (1998).
5. Chang and Velasco (1998) apply this model to various combinations of currency and depositor guarantee arrangements.
6. The current acccount deficit indicates the rate at which a country is borrowing from abroad.
7. Before the Mexican crisis in 1994, the extent of real appreciation had been estimated to as much as 30 per cent (Edwards 1998).
8. The "traded" sectors of an economy are involved in the production of goods and services that can be exported or which compete with imports. These include tourism services, the processing of commodities for exportation, manufactured exports, and import-substituting products. "Non-traded"

products and services are produced and consumed in the economy and against which products and services produced abroad cannot compete. An example is the construction industry; another example is the provision of basic services such as retailing of consumer food and goods, and the supply of electricity, gas and water.

9. For example, in the centrally planned economies trade, banking, insurance and other financial services accounted for a much lower share of GDP and total employment than in market economies.
10. Hungary, which had been in the international markets much earlier than other centrally planned economies, did not have access to any debt forgiveness. Hungary has not succumbed to the debt crisis.
11. Hölscher (1997) makes a similar argument with respect to EE countries drawing on the West German experience with undervalued mark in the 1950s.
12. This strategy also required leaning steadily against the Balassa-Samuelson pressure toward real exchange appreciation.
13. "Transformational recession" is the loss in output and increase in unemployment during transition that occurs mainly because inefficient and uncompetitive production units have to be closed so that more sustainable economic activities can take their place. The reduction in output may be aggravated by poor economic policies.
14. As they say in Russia, "Devaluation cannot be stolen."
15. "CIS" refers to the states of the Commonwealth of Independent States whose membership includes most of the federated states under the old Soviet Union. Trade with "non-CIS" states refers to trade with the West, the Baltic states that had been previously been part of the Soviet Union, the EE countries, and the rest of the world.
16. See (Popov 1996 *a*, *b* and 1998*b*).
17. This argument was also developed in the newspaper articles. See: "Growth Strategy", *Segodnya*, 14 March 1996 (in Russian); "The Currency Crisis Is Possible in Russia", *Finansoviye Izvestiya*, 30 October 1997 (in Russian); "An Emerging Economy's

Unaffordable Luxury", *Financial Times*, 11 Dec. 1997; "What Exchange Rate of the Ruble Is Needed for Russia?", *Nezavisimaya Gazeta*, 21 May 1998 (in Russian); "Arithmetic of Devaluation: Why Do We Need a Rate of 12 Roubles per Dollar", *Nezavisimaya Gazeta*, June 1998 Supplement (in Russian).

18. The other major proponent of the exchange rate based stabilization and also the former adviser of the Russian Government, Anders Aslund, pretty much like IMF, continued to deny the need to devalue even in July (his article "Don't Devalue the Ruble" in the *Moscow Times*, 7 July 1998).
19. This was a sharp contrast to the Mexican situation in the second half of 1994. As in Russia, the value of outstanding short-term government debt exceeded the amount of foreign exchange reserves. But unlike Russian GKOs, Mexican *tesobonos* were denominated in dollars, not in national currency, so devaluation of the peso could not and did not decrease the dollar value of the debt.
20. Sberbank had accounted for 75 per cent of all household deposits savings.
21. In recent years the plan was suggested by Hanke, Jonung and Schuler (1993). Among other things, the book tells an interesting story of the currency board in Northern Russia in 1918–20, during the period of the Civil War. It was set up by the British occupational forces and designed by J. M. Keynes, then a Treasury official responsible for war finance.
22. Measured conventionally and therefore not including the soaring asset and property prices which had been fed by the lending boom.
23. This is also argued in Montes (1998*a*).
24. This implies that if the problem is export competitiveness, the pressure on China to devalue now is that much greater, since the Asian currencies have fallen by over 30 per cent. However, it does not justify why these currencies have fallen so low.
25. Unlike in Latin America or in Russia, the exchange rate was not used as a anchor to fight inflation in Asia, except for Singapore in which exchange appreciation is the main instrument for controlling inflation. The unsustainably strong

peg was a key to the "tablita" era in Argentina, Chile and Uruguay in the early 1980s and is a harder sell on Asian economies.

26. Montes (1998) discusses the guarantees that are implicit in financial systems. Krugman's (1998) model of the Asian crisis also relies heavily on the operation of implicit guarantees.
27. Indonesia did have Dutch-style bankruptcy laws in place before the crisis, but these had never been tested.
28. The U.S. Government publicly supported early liquidity injection as a response to the Russian negotiations with the IMF in early July 1998; as the negotiations with the IMF dragged on, the Clinton Administration issued a public statement to the effect that it was time for the negotiations to come to an end. In five days, a new Russian IMF package, double the size that had been discussed publicly, of $22.5 billion was finalized. This package unravelled in three weeks. In October 1998, the U.S. Treasury strongly supported a $40.5 billion package for Brazil that was predicated mainly on the early injection of liquidity and no devaluation, just like the Russian package. The contrast with the Indonesian case is indeed stark.
29. In interpreting IMF programmes, private fund managers seemed to be suffering from the syndrome of being "more Catholic than the Pope" as explained in Montes (1998, p.xxviii).
30. After their accession to the OECD, Belgium and France took at least 15 years to achieve fully convertible capital accounts. Korea's planned accession was three times faster, but all would be set right upon the completion of the current IMF programme.
31. Chile began with a 15 per cent reserve requirement and this was increased to 30 per cent after one year. In the wake of the Asian crisis which reduced copper prices and increased Chile's requirement for international financing, Chile recently reduced the requirement to 10 per cent.

# References

Åslund A. "The Case for Radical Reform". *Journal of Democracy* 5, no. 4 (October 1994).

Bardacke, Ted. "Origins: The Day the Miracle Came to an End". *Financial Times*, 12 January 1998 (http://www.ft.com/hippocampus/v78b12.htm).

Bofinger, P., H. Flassbeck and L. Hoffmann. "Orthodox Money-Based Stabilization (OMBS) versus Heterodox Exchange Rate-Based Stabilization (HERBS): the Case of Russia, the Ukraine and Kazakhstan". *Economic Systems* 21, no. 1 (March 1997): 1–33.

Bond, Timothy James. "Capital Flows to Asia: The Role of Monetary Policy". Paper presented at the IIASA Conference on Financial Flows to Transition Economies, Laxenburg, Austria, 9–10 May 1997.

Bruno, Michael and William Easterly. "Inflation Crisis and Long-Run Growth". Unpublished. World Bank 1995.

Bruno, Michael. "Does Inflation Really Lower Growth?" *Finance and Development,* September 1995.

Calvo, Guillermo and Enrique G. Mendoza. "Petty Crime and Cruel Punishment: Lessons from the Mexican Debacle". *AEA Papers and Proceedings,* May 1996, pp.170–73.

Chang, Roberto and Andres Velasco. "Financial Fragility and the Exchange Rate Regime". Federal Reserve Bank of Atlanta Working Paper 97–16, November 1997.

Desai, Padma. "Russia". In *Going Global: The Transition from Plan to Marhot in the World Economy*, edited by Padma Desai, pp. 317–51. Cambridge: The MIT Press, 1997.

Edwards, Sebastian. "The Mexican Peso Crisis: How Much Did We Know? When Did We Know It?" *World Economy 1998*, pp. 1–29.

Feldstein, Martin. "Refocusing the IMF". *Foreign Affairs,* March–April 1998.

Grafe, C. and C. Wyplosz. "The Real Exchange Rate in Transition Economies". Paper presented at the Third Dubrovnik Conference On Transition Economies in Dubrovnik, Croatia, 25–28 June 1997.

Griffith-Jones, Stephany. "Causes and Lessons of the Mexican Peso Crisis". Working paper No. 132, WIDER/UNU, 1997.

Grobar, Lisa M. "The Effect of Real Exchange Rate Uncertainty on LDC Manufactured Exports". *Journal of Development Economics* 4, no. 1 (1993): pp. 36–76.

Halpern L. and C. Wyplosz. "Equilibrium Exchange Rates in Transition Economies". *IMF Staff Papers* 44, no. 4 (December 1997): 430–61.

Hanke S., L. Jonung and K. Schule. *Russian Currency and Finance: A Currency Board Approach to Reform*. New York: Routledge, 1993.

Howell, Michael. "Asia's 'Victorian' Financial Crisis". Paper presented at the Conference on the East Asian Economic Crisis, Institute for Development Studies at the University of Sussex, 13–14 July 1998.

Hölscher, J. "Economic Dynamism in Transition Economies: Lessons from Germany". *Communist Economies and Economic Transformation* 9, no. 2 (1997): 173–81.

Ito, Takatoshi. "Capital Flows: Macroeconomic Responses, Capital Controls and Moral Hazard". Manuscript. Hitotsubashi University, 4 May 1998.

Kaminsky, Graciela and Carmen M. Reinhart. "The Twin Crises: The Causes of Banking and Balance-of-Payments

Problems". International Finance Discussion Paper No. 544. Washington: Board of Governors of the Federal Reserve, March 1996.

Krugman, P. "A Model of Balance of Payments Crises". *Journal of Money, Credit, and Banking* 11 (1979), pp. 311–25.

Krugman, P. "Currency Crises" (prepared for NBER conference, October 1997). http://web.mit.edu/krugman/www/crises.html

Krugman, P. "What Happened to Asia?" January 1998. Http://web.mit.edu/krugman/www/DISINTER.html

Kwan, C. H. "Asia's Currency Crisis and Its Impact on the Japanese Economy". Tokyo: Japan Development Bank. December 1997.

McKinnon, Ronald I. and Huw Pill. "International Overborrowing: A Decomposition of Credit and Currency Risks". Manuscript. Department of Economics, Stanford University, 1998.

Montiel, Peter J. and Carmen M. Reinhart. "The Dynamics of Capital Movements to Emerging Economies During the 1990s". Manuscript. United Nations University/World Institute for Development Economics Research (UNU/WIDER). July 1996.

Montes, Manuel F. "Country Responses to Massive Capital Flows". United Nations University/World Institute for Development Economics Research (UNU/WIDER) Working Paper No. 121, Helsinki, September 1996.

Montes, Manuel F. "The Economic Miracle in a Haze". In *Growing Pains: ASEAN's Economic and Political Challenges*, Asia Society Update, edited by Manuel F. Montes, Kevin F.F. Quiqley, and Donald E. Weatherbee. New York: The Asia Society, 1997.

Montes, Manuel F. *The Currency Crisis in Southeast Asia*. Updated edition, Singapore: Institute of Southeast Asian Studies, 1998*a*.

Montes, Manuel F. "Global Lessons of the Economic Crisis in

Asia". *Asia Pacific Issues*, no. 35, East-West Center, Honolulu, Hawaii, March 1998*b*.

Montes, Manuel F. "The Philippines as an Unwitting Participant in the Asian Economic Crisis". Manuscript. Institute of Southeast Asian Studies, Singapore, March 1998*c*.

Montes, Manuel F. "Three Complications to Asian Economic Recovery". Manuscript. Institute of Southeast Asian Studies, Singapore, June 1998*d*.

Montes, Manuel F. and Muhammad Ali Abdusalamov. "Indonesia: Reaping the Market". In *Tigers in Trouble*, ed. by Jomo K.S. (Bangkok: White Lotus, 1998), pp. 162–80.

Nekipelov, A. "The Nature of Russia's Economic Catastrophe — An Alternative Diagnosis". *Transition. The Newsletter About Reforming Economies*, October 1998.

Nuti, Mario. "Inflation, Interest and Exchange Rates in the transition". *Economics of Transition* 4, no 1 (1996): 137–58.

Polak, Jacques J. "Monetary Analysis of Income Formation and Payments Problems". *International Monetary Fund Staff Papers* no. 4 (November 1957), pp. 1–50.

Popov, V. "Inflation During Transition: Is Russia's Case Special". *Acta Slavica Iaponica*, Tomus XIV, 1996*a*, Sapporo, Japan, pp. 59–75.

Popov, V. *A Russian Puzzle. What Makes Russian Economic Transformation a Special Case*. WIDER/UNU, RFA 29, 1996*b*.

Popov, V. "Lessons from Currency Crisis in South East Asia". *Voprosy Ekonomiky*, no. 12 (1997) (in Russian).

Popov, V. "Investment in Transition Economies: Factors of Change and Implications for Performance". *Journal of East-West Business* 4, no. 1/2 (1998*a*).

Popov, V. "Preparing Russian Economy for the World Market Integration". In *Regionalisation and Globalisation in the Modern World Economy*, ed. by A. Fernandez Jilberto and Andre Mommen, pp. 86–127. London: Routledge 1998*b*.

Popov, V. "Will Russia Achieve Fast Economic Growth?". *Communist Economies and Economic Transformation* no. 4, 1998*c*.

Popov, V. "The Financial System in Russia as Compared to Other Transition Economies: The Anglo- American versus The German-Japanese Model". *Comparative Economic Studies,* no. 4, 1998*d*.

Popov, V. "Explaining the Magnitude of the Transformational Recession". *Comparative Economic Studies* (forthcoming 1999).

Reisen, Helmut. "Domestic Causes of Currency Crises: Policy Lessons for Crisis Avoidance". Paper presented at the Conference on the East Asian Economic Crisis, Institute for Development Studies at the University of Sussex, 13–14 July 1998.

Rivlin, Alice. "Lessons Drawn form the Asian Financial Crisis". Reprinted in the *BIS Review* 41, 13 May 1998.

Sachs J. "Russia's Struggle with Stabilization: Conceptual Issues and Evidence". A paper prepared for the World Bank's Annual Conference on Development Economics. Washington, D.C., 28–29 April 1994.

Sachs J. *Why Russia Has Failed to Stabilize*. Working Paper No.103, Stockholm Institute of East European Economics, 1995.

Sachs, J., A. Tornell and A. Velasco. "Financial Crises in Emerging Markets: The Lessons from 1995." *Brookings Papers on Economic Activity* 1 (19960: 147–98.

Santiprabhob, V. *Bank Soundness and Currency Board Arrangements: Issues and Experience*. IMF Paper on Policy Analysis and Assessment, December 1997.

Shmelev, N. and V. Popov. *The Turning Point: Revitalizing the Soviet Economy*. New York: Doubleday, 1989.

Siamwalla, Ammar. "What Went Wrong". *Bangkok Post,* 12 November 1997.

Soros, George. "George Soros: Avoiding a Breakdown". *Financial Times*, 31 December 1997.

Stiglitz, Joseph. "More Instruments and Broader Goals: Moving Toward the Post-Washington Consensus". UNU/WIDER Annual Lecture. Helsinki:WIDER/UNU, 1998.

Subcommittee on Asian Financial and Capital Markets of the Committee on Foreign Exchange Transactions (SAFCM). "Lessons from the Asian Currency Crises - Risks Related to Short-term Capital Movements and the '21st Century-Type' Currency Crisis". Tokyo, Japan, 19 May 1998.

World Bank. *The East Asian Miracle*. New York: Oxford University Press, 1993.

World Bank. *From Plan to Market. World Development Report*, NY: Oxford University Press, 1996.

World Bank. *The State in A Changing World. World Development Report*, NY: Oxford University Press, 1997.

Zettermeyer J. and D. Citrin. *Stabilization: fixed versus flexible exchangc rates. Policy experiences and issues in the Baltics, Russian and other countries of the former Soviet Union*, Washington, DC: IMF, 1995.

## STATISTICAL SOURCES

Asian Development Bank. *Asian Development Outlook* 1997 and 1998.

European Bank for Reconstruction and Development. *Transition Report 1995*. London: EBRD, 1995.

European Bank for Reconstruction and Development. *Transition Report 1996*. London: EBRD, 1996.

European Bank for Reconstruction and Development. *Transition Report Update 1997*. London: EBRD, 1997.

Goskomstat. *Narodnoye Khozyaistvo SSSR* (National Economy of the USSR), *Rossiysky Statistichesky Yezhegodnik* (Russian Statistical Yearbook) and monthly publications for various years. Moscow.

IMF. *International Financial Statistics,* Washington, DC, 1996.
*PlanEcon*. Washington, DC, various issues.
World Bank. *World Development Indicators 1997.*
World Bank. *World Development Indicators 1998.*

# Index

## ABOUT THE AUTHORS

MANUEL F. MONTES, Ph.D., is an Associate Senior Fellow at the Institute of Southeast Asian Studies (ISEAS), Singapore and Senior Fellow, East-West Center in Honolulu, Hawai'i. In 1996–97, he was a co-director of the project "Short-term Capital Movements and Balance of Payments Crises" of the United Nations University/World Institute for Development Economics Research (UNU/WIDER) in Helsinki, Finland. He held the Chair in Money and Banking at the School of Economics, University of the Philippines in Manila. Among his recent publications are: *The Currency Crisis in Southeast Asia,* Updated Edition (1998); "Global Lessons of the Economic Crisis in Asia", *Asia-Pacific Issues*, no. 35 (1998); "Indonesia: Reaping the Market" in *Tigers in Trouble* edited by Jomo K.S. (1998).

VLADIMIR POPOV, Ph.D., is Sector Head at the Academy of the National Economy in Moscow, Russia. In 1998–99 he was a Visiting Professor at Queen's University (Kingston) and Carleton University (Ottawa) in Canada. In 1996-98 he was co-directing a project "Transition Strategies, Alternatives and Outcomes" of the United Nations University World Institute for Development Economics Research (UNU/WIDER) in Helsinki, Finland. His recent articles include: "Explaining the Magnitude of Transformational Recession", *Comparative Economic Studies* (forthcoming 1999); "Investment in Transition Economies: Factors of Change and Implications for Performance", *Journal of East-West Business* 4, no. 1/2 (1998); "The Financial System in Russia as Compared to the other Transition Economies: The Anglo-American Versus the German-Japanese Model", *Comparative Economic Studies*, no. 4 (1998); "Will Russia Achieve Fast Economic Growth?" *Communist Economies and Economic Transformation*, no. 4 (1998).